Cambridge Primary

Hodder Cambridge Primary
Maths

Workbook

Stage 2

Catherine Casey

Series editors: Mike Askew
and Paul Broadbent

HODDER
EDUCATION
AN HACHETTE UK COMPANY

Acknowledgements

With warm thanks to Jennifer Peek for her help in shaping and developing this title.

The Publisher is extremely grateful to the following schools for their comments and feedback during the development of this series:

Avalon Heights World Private School, Ajman

The Oxford School, Dubai

Al Amana Private School, Sharjah

British International School, Ajman

Wesgreen International School, Sharjah

As Seeb International School, Al Khoud.

Every effort has been made to trace all copyright holders, but if any have been inadvertently overlooked the Publishers will be pleased to make the necessary arrangements at the first opportunity.

Although every effort has been made to ensure that website addresses are correct at time of going to press, Hodder Education cannot be held responsible for the content of any website mentioned in this book. It is sometimes possible to find a relocated web page by typing in the address of the home page for a website in the URL window of your browser.

Hachette UK's policy is to use papers that are natural, renewable and recyclable products and made from wood grown in sustainable forests. The logging and manufacturing processes are expected to conform to the environmental regulations of the country of origin.

Orders: please contact Bookpoint Ltd, 130 Milton Park, Abingdon, Oxon OX14 4SB. Telephone: (44) 01235 827720. Fax: (44) 01235 400454. Lines are open from 9.00–5.00, Monday to Saturday, with a 24-hour message answering service. You can also order through our website www.hoddereducation.com

© Catherine Casey 2017

Published by Hodder Education

An Hachette UK Company

Carmelite House, 50 Victoria Embankment, London EC4Y 0DZ

Impression number   1 2 3 4 5

Year   2021 2020 2019 2018 2017

Cover illustration by Steve Evans

Illustrations by Karen Ahlschläger, Jeanne du Plessis and Anna-Marie Brink

Typeset in FS Albert 17/19 by DTP Impressions

Printed in Great Britain by Hobbs the Printers Ltd, Totton, Hampshire SO40 3WX

A catalogue record for this title is available from the British Library

9781471884597

Contents

Term 1

Term 2

Term 3

Unit 1 Number and problem solving

Can you remember?

a One less than 6 is ☐.

b Ten less than 32 is ☐.

c One more than 14 is ☐.

d Ten more than 8 is ☐.

Numbers to 100

1 Match the number names to the two-digit numbers.

fourteen   ㉕

twenty-five   ㊱

thirty-six   ⑭

forty-seven   ㊼

2 Fill in the missing numbers.

1	2	3	4	5	6	7		9	10
11		13	14	15	16	17	18	19	20
21	22	23	24		26	27	28	29	
31	32	33	34	35	36		38	39	40
41	42	43		45	46	47	48	49	50
	52	53	54	55		57	58	59	60
61	62	63	64	65	66	67	68	69	
71	72	73		75	76	77	78	79	80
81	82	83	84		86	87		89	90
91	92		94	95	96	97	98	99	100

3 Take a handful of items like crayons, pebbles, shells, paper-clips or dried pasta.

Count them in twos, fives and tens. How many are there?

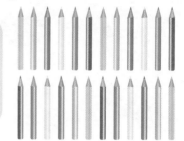

> **Example**
> I counted in twos.
> There are 24 crayons.

I counted in _____. There are _____.

I counted in _____. There are _____.

I counted in _____. There are _____.

4 Draw the frog jumps on the number line.
Circle each number the frog lands on.

a Count in **twos**.

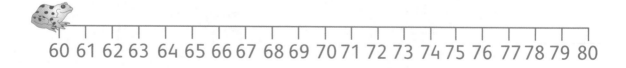

40   41   ⟨42⟩   43   44   45   46   47   48   49   50

b Count in **fives**.

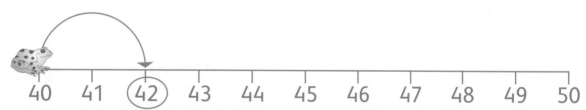

60 61 62 63 64 65 66 67 68 69 70 71 72 73 74 75 76 77 78 79 80

c Count in **tens**.

30   35   40   45   50   55   60   65   70   75   80

Comparing numbers

1 Draw a circle around the bigger number.

a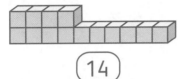

⓵14   17

b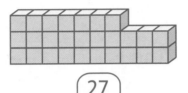

27   24

c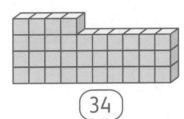

34   37

2 Fill in the missing numbers.

a

b

3 Round the numbers to the nearest multiple of 10.

a [ ] ◀—— 53   b [ ] ◀—— 71

c 47 ——▶ [ ]   d 89 ——▶ [ ]

4 Draw a picture of five children standing in a line.
The **1st** child is wearing a blue T-shirt.
The **2nd** child is the tallest.
The **3rd** child is wearing a hat.
The **4th** child is wearing a green T-shirt.
The **5th** child is the shortest.

5 The pictures of the plant are mixed up. Put the pictures in the correct order. Start with the seed that you plant. The first one has been done for you.

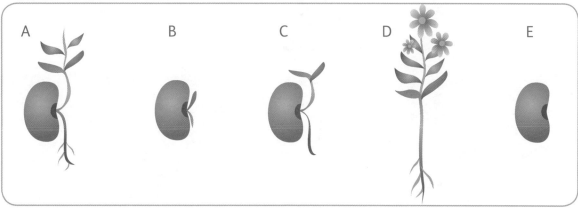

A   B   C   D   E

1st: Picture [E]   2nd: Picture [ ]

3rd: Picture [ ]   4th: Picture [ ]

5th: Picture [ ]

Number and place value

 Make your own place value apparatus.

You will need
- a packet of drinking straws
- string/ribbon/elastic bands

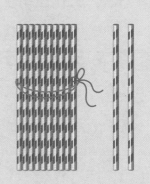

Method
Make tens: Count out ten straws.
Tie them together with string.
Repeat four times.
Make ones: Use individual straws.

Now make these numbers.

a 13   **b** 14   **c** 15   **d** 23   **e** 24

f 34   **g** 43   **h** 44   **i** 45

 a Sort the numbers. Write them in the Venn diagram.

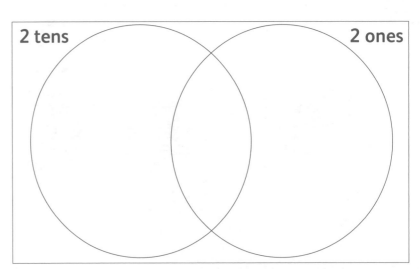

22 42 52 21 32 23 25 26

2 tens   2 ones

b Choose your own numbers. Write each number in the correct place in the Venn diagram.

3 Guess the numbers.

a ◯

I think of a number. I add 10.
The answer is 13.
What number did I start with?

b ◯

I think of a number. I subtract 10.
The answer is 13.
What number did I start with?

c ◯

I think of a number. I add 1.
The answer is 76.
What number did I start with?

d ◯

I think of a number. I subtract 1.
The answer is 76.
What number did I start with?

e Write your own number problem.

_____

_____

_____

_____

Self-assessment

Unit 1 Number and problem solving

😊 I understand this well.

😐 I understand this, but I need more practice.

☹️ I don't understand this.

I need more help with …

_____

_____

_____

Self-check statements	😊	😐	☹️
I can read and write two-digit numbers.			
I can count on and back in ones and tens.			
I can count in twos, fives and tens and show the jumps along a number line.			
I can write any missing number on a number line marked off in multiples of 10.			
I can use 1st, 2nd, 3rd, and so on, to show the order of objects.			
I know what each digit means in two-digit numbers.			
I can work out 1 or 10 more or less than any number.			
I can round two-digit numbers to the nearest multiple of ten.			

Unit 2 Geometry and problem solving

Can you remember?

Name these 3-D shapes.

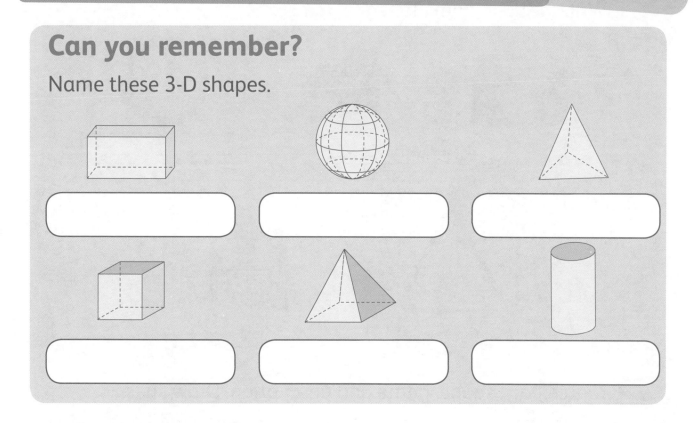

2-D shapes and symmetry

1 Match each picture to its shape name. Draw lines.

| circle | pentagon | hexagon | rectangle | square | triangle |

2 Tick each shape that has a line of symmetry.

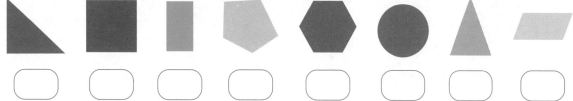

3 Write a shape name for each item.

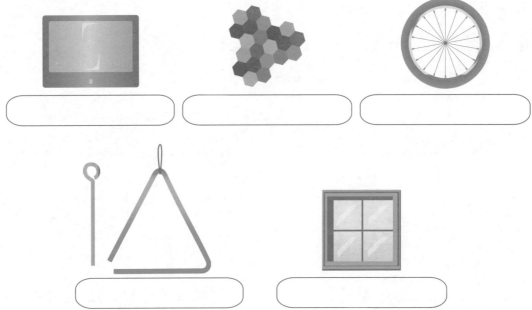

4 Match each shape, name and description. Draw lines.

three sides and three corners	▪	square
four sides and four corners	⬠	pentagon
four sides and four corners	▮	rectangle
five sides and five corners	▲	triangle
six sides and six corners	⬡	hexagon

5 Tick each shape with three corners.

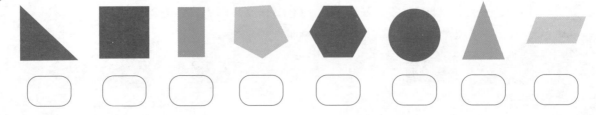

6 Draw a line of symmetry on each shape.

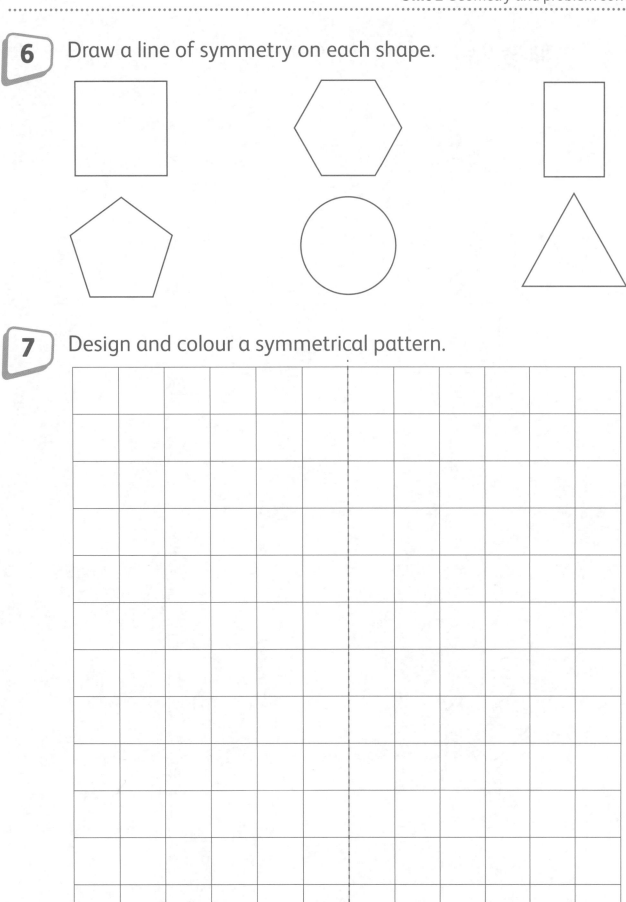

7 Design and colour a symmetrical pattern.

Complete the symmetrical pictures.

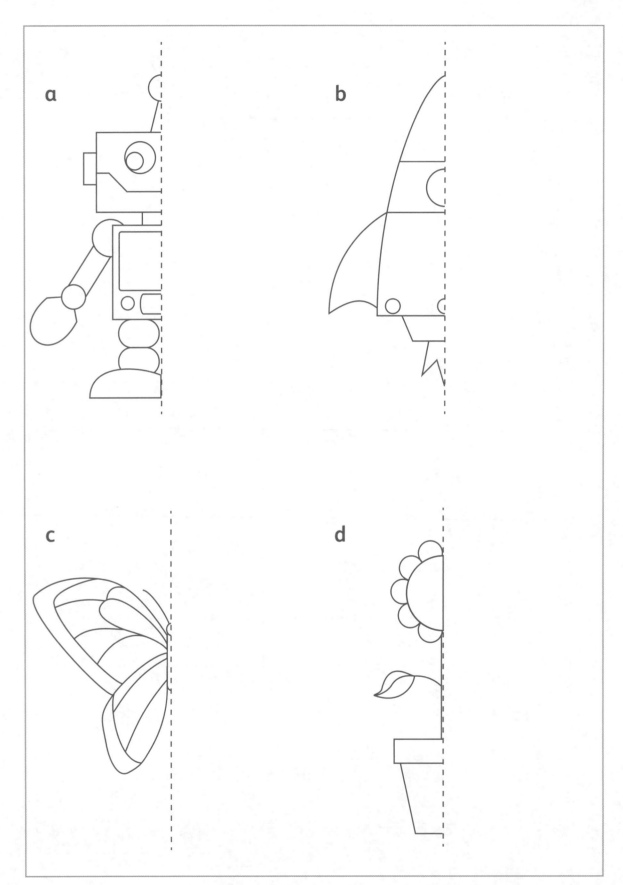

Shapes around me

1 Label the picture. Choose the words from the list.

| sphere | cylinder | pyramid |
| cuboid | prism | cone |

You will need
colouring pencils

2 Colour the picture.

a Colour the spheres blue.

b Colour the cylinder green.

c Colour the cuboid orange

d Colour the pyramid purple.

e Colour the cone yellow.

f Colour the prism red.

3 What shapes are they describing?

Draw the shape.

My shape has 6 square faces, 8 vertices and 12 edges.
What is my shape?

Draw the shape.

My shape has 1 square face, 4 triangular faces, 5 vertices and 8 edges.
What is my shape?

4 Choose four 3-D shapes with straight edges.
Complete the table. Describe the four shapes.

Shape	Number of faces	Number of vertices	Number of edges

Self-assessment

Unit 2 Geometry and problem solving

😃 I understand this well.

😐 I understand this, but I need more practice.

☹️ I don't understand this.

I need more help with ...

_____

_____

_____

Self-check statements	😃	😐	☹️
I can look at pictures of 2-D shapes and name them.			
I can sort sets of 2-D shapes in different ways.			
I can describe different shapes and talk about their properties.			
I can draw a line of symmetry on a shape.			
I can complete a symmetrical picture by drawing the 'other half'.			
I can name 3-D shapes.			
I can find and describe shapes around me.			
I can describe the 2-D shapes on the faces of 3-D shapes.			

Unit 3 Number and problem solving

Can you remember?

$6 + \boxed{} = 20$ $5 + \boxed{} = 20$ $4 + \boxed{} = 20$

$20 - \boxed{} = 15$ $20 - \boxed{} = 14$ $20 - \boxed{} = 13$

Number facts

1   Make 10 in different ways. Fill in the missing numbers.

a 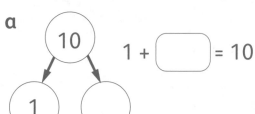 $1 + \boxed{} = 10$

b 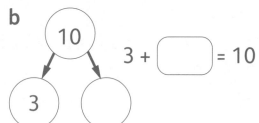 $3 + \boxed{} = 10$

c 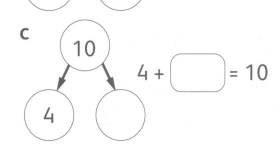 $4 + \boxed{} = 10$

d 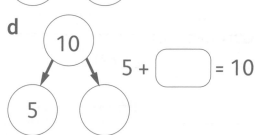 $5 + \boxed{} = 10$

2   Use a different colour for each number. Shade in the blocks to match each number sentence.

a $6 + 2 = \boxed{}$

b $5 + 4 = \boxed{}$

c $3 + 4 = \boxed{}$

d $7 + 2 = \boxed{}$

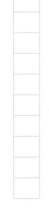

Remember you can add in any order!

3 Match the flower to the correct pot to total 100.

4 Choose two items from the picture to balance each scale.

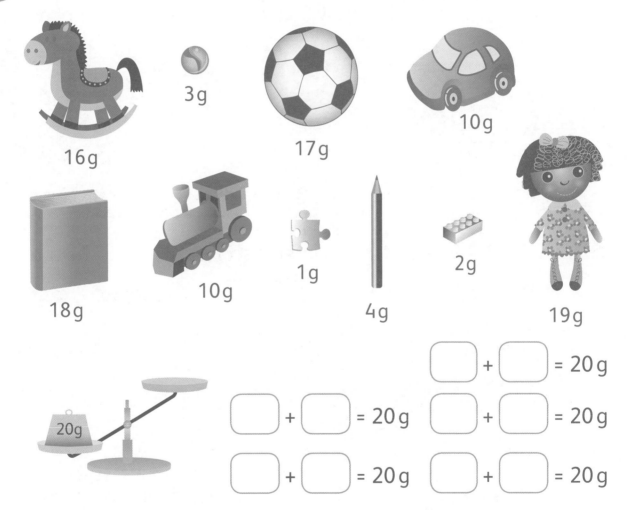

16g

3g

17g

10g

18g

10g

1g

4g

2g

19g

☐ + ☐ = 20 g

☐ + ☐ = 20 g   ☐ + ☐ = 20 g

20g

☐ + ☐ = 20 g   ☐ + ☐ = 20 g

5 Fill in the missing numbers.

1 + 7 = ☐   4 + ☐ = 7   13 + 6 = ☐

2 + ☐ = 15   11 + 5 = ☐   14 + ☐ = 17

Addition and subtraction

1 Write down six different ways to complete the boxes.

◯ + ◯ + ◯ = 9   ◯ + ◯ + ◯ = 9

◯ + ◯ + ◯ = 9   ◯ + ◯ + ◯ = 9

◯ + ◯ + ◯ = 9   ◯ + ◯ + ◯ = 9

2 The children are playing a game. Each child tries to throw a hoop over the cones. They take turns to throw three hoops each.

Look out for doubles or number bonds to 10.

a The table shows the children's scores. Work out the totals.

Name	1st hoop	2nd hoop	3rd hoop	Total
Tessa	7	7	3	
Bruno	5	5	7	
Jade	3	5	7	
Manuel	3	3	3	

b Who has the lowest score?

c Write the different scores you could get with four hoops.

3 Draw the jumps on the number lines. Complete the number sentences.

Remember to do subtraction in the order it appears.

a
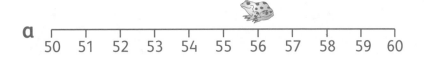
50 51 52 53 54 55 56 57 58 59 60

56 − 3 =

b
40 41 42 43 44 45 46 47 48 49 50

48 − 2 =

c
70 71 72 73 74 75 76 77 78 79 80

77 − 5 =

d
80 81 82 83 84 85 86 87 88 89 90

84 − 3 =

4 Gabriel had 38 marbles.
He gave six to his friend.
How many does he have left?

5 Sofia had 45 colouring pencils.
She lost three pencils.
How many does she have left?

6 Julio thought of a number.
He took away four. He has 83 left.
What number did Julio start with?

Multiplication

1

Circle the multiples of 2.	Circle the multiples of 10.
20 16 18 15 12 13 17 14 11	42 50 35 100 57 40 70 30 83 90 61 60 20 78 80

2 Colour the multiples of 5.

1	2	3	4	5	6	7	8	9	10
11	12	13	14	15	16	17	18	19	20
21	22	23	24	25	26	27	28	29	30
31	32	33	34	35	36	37	38	39	40
41	42	43	44	45	46	47	48	49	50
51	52	53	54	55	56	57	58	59	60
61	62	63	64	65	66	67	68	69	70
71	72	73	74	75	76	77	78	79	80
81	82	83	84	85	86	87	88	89	90
91	92	93	94	95	96	97	98	99	100

3 a Colour the balloons with
    even numbers blue.
  b Colour the balloons with
    odd numbers yellow.

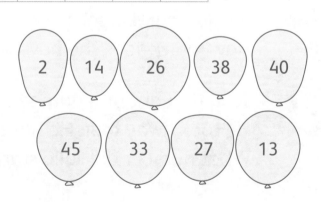

Draw dots to show each repeated addition.
The first one has been started for you.

a (••••) (••••) (••••)

4 + 4 + 4 = ( )   4 × 3 = ( )

b ( ) ( ) ( ) ( )

3 + 3 + 3 + 3 = ( )   3 × 4 = ( )

c ( ) ( ) ( )

2 + 2 + 2 = ( )   2 × 3 = ( )

 Complete the number sentences for each array.

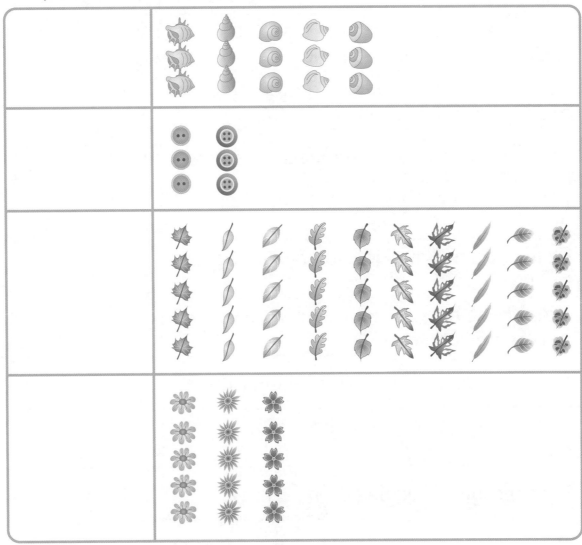

Self-assessment

Unit 3 Number and problem solving

☺	I understand this well.
😐	I understand this, but I need more practice.
☹	I don't understand this.

I need more help with …

_____

_____

_____

Self-check statements	☺	😐	☹
I know the number bonds to 10.			
I can use number bonds to 10 to find multiples of 10 that total 100.			
I can work out the addition and subtraction facts for all numbers to 20.			
I can add sets of small numbers together.			
I can use the +, – and = signs when I add and subtract.			
I can add small numbers to any number up to 100.			
I can show that multiplication is the same as repeated addition.			
I can use an array to show a multiplication.			
I can recognise some multiples of 2, 5 and 10.			
I can recognise odd and even numbers.			

Unit 4 Measure and problem solving

Can you remember?

| | months in a year | | days in a week |
| | minutes in an hour | | seconds in a minute |

Money

1 Match each purse or hand to the correct amount of money. The first one has been done for you.

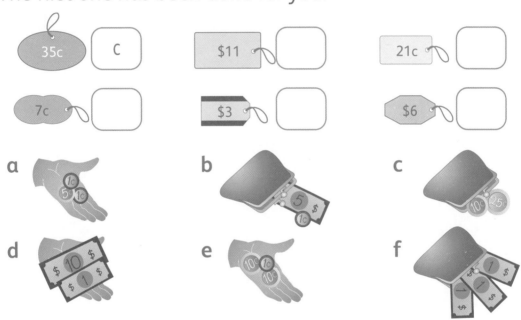

2 Tick three coins to make each total.

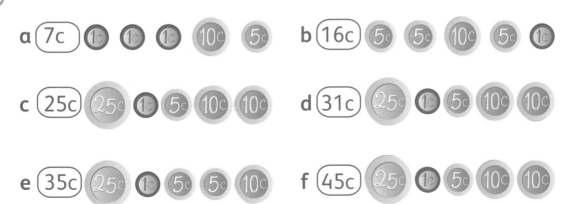

3 How much do you pay for stationery?

Items bought	Work out the total cost	Draw notes and coins to make the amount
	$2 + $6 = $8	

4 How much change do you get from $20?

a

b

c

d

Measuring length

1   **a** Estimate the length of each line.
     b Use a ruler to measure the length of each line in centimetres.

You will need
a ruler

A ─────────────────────

B ─────

C ──────────────

D ───────────────────────

E ───

F ────────────────

G ─

H ──────────

Remember to place the ruler with the 0 cm at the beginning of the line you are measuring.

Line	Estimate	Measurement
A		
B		
C		
D		
E		
F		
G		
H		

2   **a** Which is the shortest line? ☐

     b Which is the longest line? ☐

     c Write the line lengths in order from shortest to longest.

3 Choose five items to measure. Complete the table.

Item	Estimate length in cm	Length in cm

4 The children practised long jump. They measured each jump.

a Victor jumped 1 cm further than Tessa. How far did he jump? Complete the table.

Carlos	87 cm
Tessa	85 cm
Victor	
Lucia	91 cm

b Who jumped the furthest?

c Whose jump was the shortest?

d Write the lengths in order from shortest to longest.

Time

1 **a** Complete the table. Fill in the missing days of the week.

Tuesday
Wednesday
Saturday

b Complete the table.
Fill in the missing months of the year.

January		March	April		June
		September			December

2 Match the lengths of time. The first one has been done for you.

24 hours		1 year
12 months		1 hour
7 days		1 minute
60 minutes		1 week
60 seconds		1 day

3 Draw the hands on each clock to show the time.

3 o'clock   5 o'clock   9 o'clock   12 o'clock

4 Draw the hands on each clock to show the time.

half past 2

half past 11

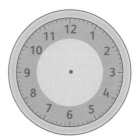
half past 6

5 Write the digital time for each clock.

6 The clock shows the time the train arrived. Write the time.

Self-assessment

Unit 4 Measure and problem solving

😊 I understand this well.

😐 I understand this, but I need more practice.

☹️ I don't understand this.

I need more help with …

_____

_____

_____

Self-check statements	😊	😐	☹️
I can recognise and name the coins and notes we use.			
I can write money amounts correctly.			
I can pay for items with different coins and notes.			
I can work out the change when I give a note.			
I can use a ruler and metre stick to measure the length of objects.			
I can compare lengths and know how long a metre is and how long a centimetre is.			
I know the difference between seconds, minutes and hours.			
I know how many days there are in a week.			
I know the days of the week and the months of the year, and can say them in order.			
I can read the time to the half-hour and use 'o'clock' and 'half past'.			

Unit 6 Number and problem solving

Can you remember?

26, 36, 46, ☐, 66, ☐, ☐

98, ☐, 78, ☐, 58, 48, ☐

33, 34, ☐, ☐, ☐, 38, ☐

Counting patterns

1 **a** Count **on** in tens.

44, ☐, ☐, ☐, ☐, ☐

45, ☐, ☐, ☐, ☐

b Count **back** in tens.

87, ☐, ☐, ☐, ☐, ☐

86, ☐, ☐, ☐, ☐, ☐

2 Letter B has a mass of 70 g.

A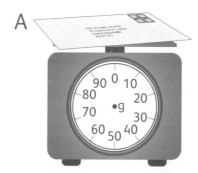

a Letter A is 10 g heavier than letter B. Letter A's mass is ☐ g.

b Letter C is 10 g lighter than letter B. Letter C's mass is ☐ g.

B  C

c Draw arrows on the scales to show the masses for letters A and C.

3 Estimate how many fish there are in the fish tanks altogether. Tick one.

10 ⬜ 30 ⬜ 50 ⬜ 100 ⬜

Remember to count in 10s, 2s or 5s.

4 Each hutch has 2 rabbits.
How many rabbits are there in ...
4 hutches? 5 hutches? 6 hutches? 7 hutches?
⬜ ⬜ ⬜ ⬜

5 The fish food costs $5 for 1 tin.
What is the cost of ...
6 tins? 7 tins? 8 tins? 9 tins?
⬜ ⬜ ⬜ ⬜

Comparing, ordering and estimating

1 Use the **<** and **>** signs to compare the numbers.

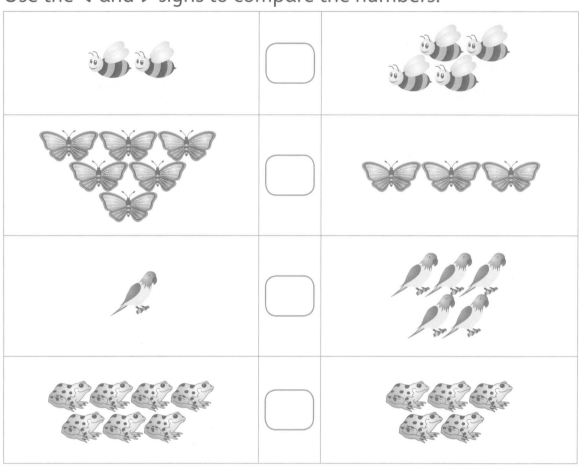

2 Draw pictures to make the sentences true.

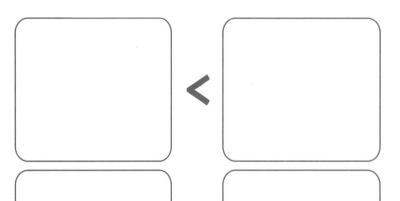

Remember **<** means 'is less than' and **>** means 'is greater than'.

3 **a** Use the < and > signs to compare the numbers.

37 ☐ 26   12 ☐ 92   34 ☐ 44

35 ☐ 53   64 ☐ 46   79 ☐ 63

b Choose numbers to complete the number sentences.

18 > ☐   36 > ☐   53 > ☐

18 < ☐   36 < ☐   53 < ☐

4 Put the pictures in order. Label them 1st, 2nd, 3rd and 4th.

a

☐   1st   ☐   ☐

b

☐   ☐   ☐   ☐

5 Write the numbers in order from smallest to biggest.

71, 24, 53, 21, 34   ☐ , ☐ , ☐ , ☐ , ☐

68, 13, 2, 93, 51   ☐ , ☐ , ☐ , ☐ , ☐

23, 6, 18, 84, 31   ☐ , ☐ , ☐ , ☐ , ☐

17, 7, 77, 47, 27   ☐ , ☐ , ☐ , ☐ , ☐

98, 99, 9, 19, 29   ☐ , ☐ , ☐ , ☐ , ☐

Number and place value

 Write the tens and ones. The first one has been done for you.

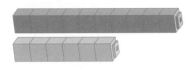

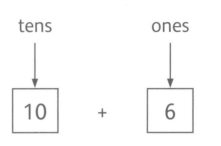

tens   ones   total

10   +   6   =   16

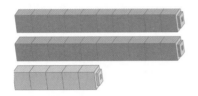

a   ⬭ + ⬭ = ⬭

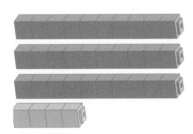

b   ⬭ + ⬭ = ⬭

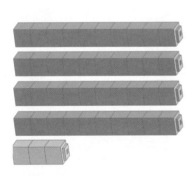

c   ⬭ + ⬭ = ⬭

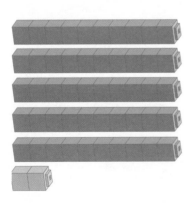

d   ⬭ + ⬭ = ⬭

2 Complete the number sentences.

Can you remember
1 more and 1 less,
10 more and 10 less?
Use your knowledge of
place value to help you.

34 + 1 = ☐

34 + 10 = ☐

34 − 1 = ☐

34 − 10 = ☐

52 + 1 = ☐

52 + 10 = ☐

52 − 1 = ☐

52 − 10 = ☐

67 − 1 = ☐

67 + 10 = ☐

67 + 1 = ☐

67 − 10 = ☐

3   **a** Rosi picked 14 apples. Matias picked 10 more apples than Rosi. How many apples did Matias pick?

14 + 10 = ☐

b Lola picked 10 apples less
than Matias.
How many apples did Lola pick?

☐

c Rashid picked 17 apples.
He ate 1 apple.
How many apples were left?

☐

d Nina had 22 apples in her basket.
She picked 1 more.
How many apples did Nina have?

☐

Self-assessment

Unit 6 Number and problem solving

😃 I understand this well.

😐 I understand this, but I need more practice.

☹ I don't understand this.

I need more help with …

_____

_____

_____

Self-check statements	😃	😐	☹
I can count on and back in ones and tens from numbers over 20.			
I can count groups of objects in twos, fives and tens.			
I can use the < and > signs to compare numbers.			
I can put numbers up to 100 in order.			
I can partition numbers into tens and ones and know what each digit means.			
I can work out 1 or 10 more or less than any number and know what happens to the digits.			

Can you remember?

Draw a table to show how many items there are.

Sorting objects and shapes

1 Sort the shapes. Draw them to complete the Carroll diagram.

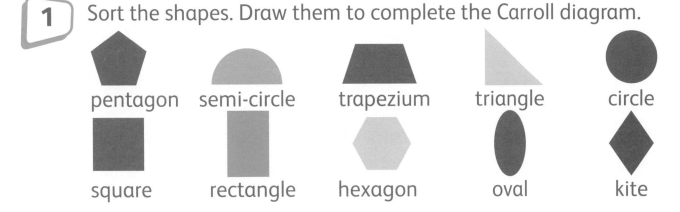

pentagon   semi-circle   trapezium   triangle   circle

square   rectangle   hexagon   oval   kite

Four sides	Not four sides

Which shapes have curved sides?

2 Sort the numbers. Write them in the Venn diagram.

50   45   52   54   40   30   35   25   20   22   18

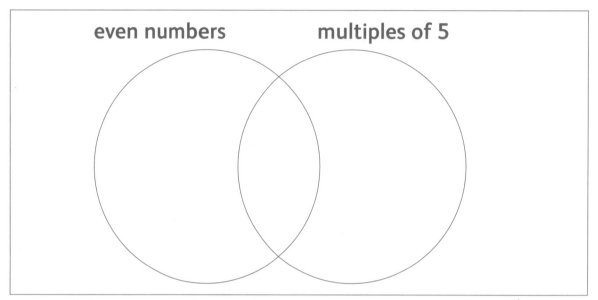

Now add six more of your own numbers.

3 Look at the Venn diagram. Write the headings in the boxes.

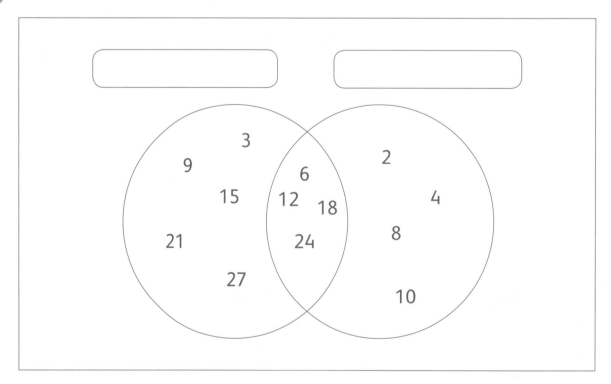

Block graphs and pictograms

1 An explorer recorded the number of animals he saw in the rainforest. He used the data to create a pictogram.

Rainforest animals		Key
Parrot	👀👀👀👀👀👀	👀
Snake	👀👀👀	= 1 animal
Tiger	👀👀👀👀👀👀👀👀👀👀👀	
Monkey	👀👀👀👀👀	
Lizard	👀👀	

Help Macie complete the table by writing in the totals.

Animal	Tally	Number
Parrot	ⅢⅠ	6
Snake	ⅢⅠ	
Tiger	Ⅲ Ⅲ Ⅰ	
Monkey	Ⅲ	
Lizard	Ⅱ	

a Which animal was most common?

b How many parrots did the explorer see?

c How many monkeys did the explorer see?

d How many more tigers than snakes did the explorer see?

e How many animals did the explorer see altogether?

2 Dylan asked his friends which shape they like best. He recorded the data in a table. Help Dylan complete the table.

Shape		Tally	Number of people
Star	★	卌 ll	7
Circle	●	卌 llll	
Square	■	lll	
Triangle	▲	卌 lll	

3 Draw a pictogram using the data Dylan collected.

Key

a Which shape is the most popular?

b Which shape is the least popular?

c How many children chose triangles?

d How many children chose stars?

4 Jade and Matias asked children how they travel to school. They started a block graph to show their data. Help them complete it.

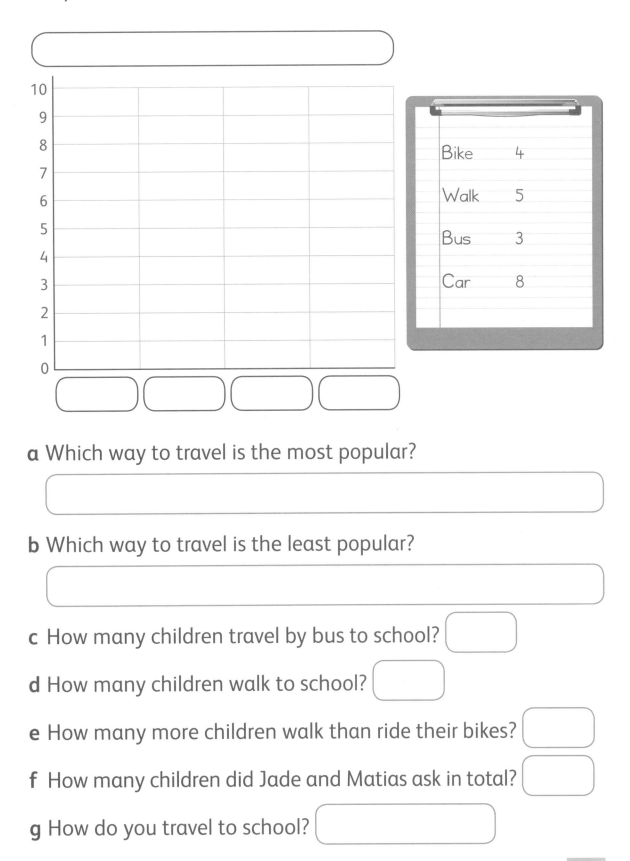

Bike   4

Walk   5

Bus   3

Car   8

a Which way to travel is the most popular?

b Which way to travel is the least popular?

c How many children travel by bus to school?

d How many children walk to school?

e How many more children walk than ride their bikes?

f How many children did Jade and Matias ask in total?

g How do you travel to school?

Unit 7 Handling data and problem solving

☺	I understand this well.
☺	I understand this, but I need more practice.
☹	I don't understand this.

I need more help with …

_____

_____

_____

Self-check statements	☺	☺	☹
I can sort sets of 2-D shapes in different ways on a Carroll diagram.			
I can sort numbers in different ways on a Venn diagram.			
I can draw a pictogram from data that has been collected.			
I can answer questions about a pictogram.			
I can draw a block graph from data that has been collected.			
I can answer questions about a block graph.			

Unit 8 Number and problem solving

Can you remember?

$1 + 19 = \boxed{}$ $6 + \boxed{} = 20$ $3 + 17 = \boxed{}$

$20 - 18 = \boxed{}$ $20 - \boxed{} = 7$ $20 - \boxed{} = 11$

Addition and subtraction

1 Fill in the missing numbers.

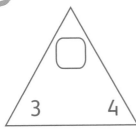

$3 + 4 = \boxed{}$

$4 + 3 = \boxed{}$

$\boxed{} - 3 = 4$

$\boxed{} - 4 = 3$

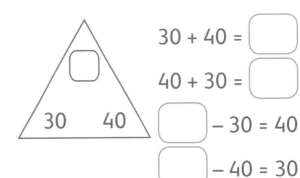

$30 + 40 = \boxed{}$

$40 + 30 = \boxed{}$

$\boxed{} - 30 = 40$

$\boxed{} - 40 = 30$

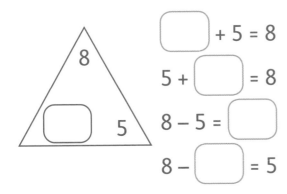

$\boxed{} + 5 = 8$

$5 + \boxed{} = 8$

$8 - 5 = \boxed{}$

$8 - \boxed{} = 5$

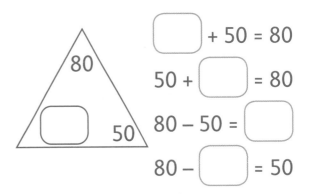

$\boxed{} + 50 = 80$

$50 + \boxed{} = 80$

$80 - 50 = \boxed{}$

$80 - \boxed{} = 50$

2 Draw jumps of ten to complete the calculations.

a $28 + 20 = \boxed{}$ ├─────────────────────┤
                                        28

b $28 + 30 = \boxed{}$ ├─────────────────────┤
                                        28

3 The children were practising high jump.

Name	1st Jump	2nd Jump
Sofia	83 cm	86 cm
Carlos	73 cm	75 cm
Bruno	81 cm	86 cm
Lucia	71 cm	75 cm
Tim	84 cm	86 cm

How much higher did each child jump on the second jump?
Count on to work out the difference. Look at the example.

Sofia: 86 cm – 83 cm = [3 cm]

83   84   85   86

Carlos: 75 – 73 = [ ]   Bruno: [ ] – [ ] = [ ]

Lucia: [ ] – [ ] = [ ]   Tim: [ ] – [ ] = [ ]

Multiplication

 1 Match each number to its double. Draw lines.

| 1 | 2 | 3 | 4 | 5 | 6 | 7 | 8 | 9 | 10 |

| 18 | 10 | 14 | 6 | 8 | 2 | 20 | 4 | 12 | 16 |

 2 A box of colouring pencils has five pencils.
Draw an array for each question.
Write the number sentences to complete the table.

Question	Draw an array	Write a number sentence
How many pencils are there in two boxes?	⬭⬭ ⬭⬭ ⬭⬭ ⬭⬭ ⬭⬭	5 × 2 = 10
How many pencils are there in three boxes?		
How many pencils are there in four boxes?		
How many pencils are there in five boxes?		
How many pencils are there in six boxes?		

Division

Jade had 28 marbles. She put them into groups of 4.
How many groups are there?

28 ÷ 4 = 7

1 Julio had 20 marbles. He put them into groups of 5.
How many groups are there?

2 Manuel had 15 toy cars. He put them in rows of 3.
How many rows were there?

3 Maya had 45 toy bricks. She built towers of 5 bricks.
How many towers did she build?

4 Match each division number sentence to its multiplication number sentence. Draw lines.

| 3 × 2 = 6 | 5 × 4 = 20 | 3 × 5 = 15 | 4 × 3 = 12 | 5 × 5 = 25 |

| 15 ÷ 3 = 5 | 6 ÷ 3 = 2 | 25 ÷ 5 = 5 | 20 ÷ 5 = 4 | 12 ÷ 4 = 3 |

5 12 ÷ 3 = ☐

13 ÷ 3 = ☐ remainder ☐

14 ÷ 3 = ☐ remainder ☐

20 ÷ 4 = ☐

21 ÷ 4 = ☐ remainder ☐

22 ÷ 4 = ☐ remainder ☐

18 ÷ 3 = ☐

19 ÷ 3 = ☐ remainder ☐

20 ÷ 3 = ☐ remainder ☐

Hint
Sometimes there are some left over when you divide. This is called the remainder!
6 ÷ 3 = 2
●●● ●●●

7 ÷ 3 = 2 remainder 1
●●● ●●● ●

6 Rosi had 16 toy bricks. She built towers of 3.
How many towers were there? ☐

How many bricks were left over? ☐

Self-assessment

Unit 8 Number and problem solving

😊 I understand this well.

😐 I understand this, but I need more practice.

☹️ I don't understand this.

I need more help with …

_____

_____

_____

Self-check statements	😊	😐	☹️
I know number bonds to 10 and pairs of numbers that total 20.			
I can add single-digit numbers to and from two-digit numbers.			
I can add and subtract multiples of 10 to and from two-digit numbers.			
I can count on to find the difference between two near numbers.			
I know all the doubles up to double 10.			
I can use an array and explain how it shows a multiplication.			
I can show how to solve word problems using pictures or objects.			
I can use grouping to show division.			
I can use the ÷ sign.			
I understand that division can leave some left over.			

Unit 9 Measure and problem solving

Can you remember?

How much money is there in each picture?

a + 10¢ + 5¢ = [ ] c   **b** $ 5 $ + $ 10 $ = $ [ ]

Money

1   Match each purse or hand to the correct amount of money.

$1.10 $10.50 $5.10 $10.25 $5.50

2   You buy fruit at the fruit stall. Complete the table.

Item bought	Note used to pay	Calculation	Your change
$4 (pineapple)	$ 5 $	5 − 4 = [ ]	$ 1 $
$3 (bananas)	$ 10 $		
$2 (coconut)	$ 10 $		
$5 (grapes)	$ 10 $		

Measuring mass

 1 Match each parcel to its mass on the scale. Draw lines.

 2 Almonds cost \$2 per 100 g. What is the mass of each of these?

160g

190g

180g

250g

170g

g

g

g

g

3 **a** Choose five items and complete the table.

Item	Estimate the mass	Weigh your item

Make sure you estimate before you weigh the item.

b Put your items in order from lightest to heaviest. Draw pictures.

lightest		←——→		heaviest

4 Use the < and > signs to compare the weights.

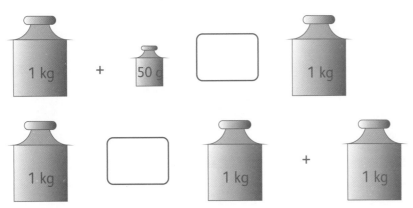

Time

1 Manuel visited his grandmother on Monday. He stayed for three days. On which day of the week did Manuel return home?

2 It is a Saturday today. Lucia's birthday is in four days' time. On which day of the week is Lucia's birthday this year?

3 Carlos posted a parcel on Wednesday to a friend.
The parcel took two days to arrive at his friend's house.
On which day of the week did the parcel arrive?

4 Match the times to the digital clocks. Draw lines.

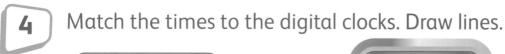

half past 10   3:00

half past 6   4:00

3 o'clock   6:30

11 o'clock   10:30

4 o'clock   11:00

5 Draw hands on the analogue clocks for the time on the digital clocks.

12:00 **3:30** **8:00**

6 Write the digital times.

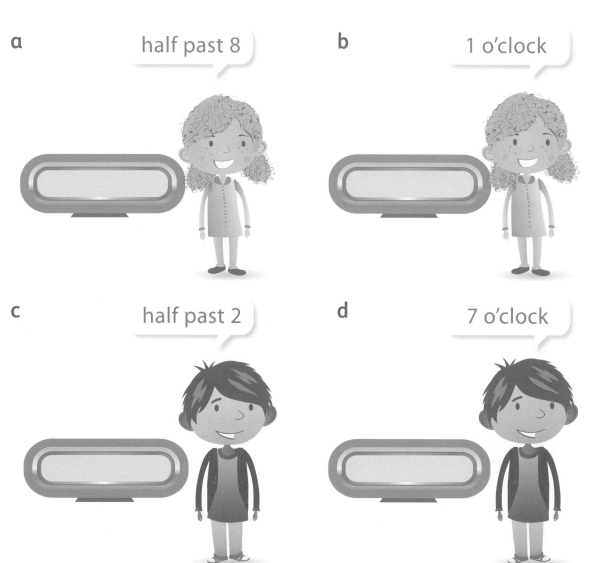

a half past 8

b 1 o'clock

c half past 2

d 7 o'clock

Self-assessment

Unit 9 Measure and problem solving

I understand this well.

I understand this, but I need more practice.

I don't understand this.

I need more help with ...

_____

_____

_____

Self-check statements			
I can pay for items with a mix of coins and notes.			
I can work out the change when I pay for an item.			
I can estimate the mass of objects and measure using non-standard units.			
I can use scales to measure the mass of objects.			
I can use grams and kilograms to compare the mass of objects.			
I know the difference between seconds, minutes and hours.			
I know how many minutes there are in an hour.			
I can read the time to the half-hour and match digital and analogue clocks.			

Unit 11 Number and problem solving

Can you remember?

1 Complete the patterns.

2, 4, ⬜, 8, 10, ⬜, ⬜

5, 10, ⬜, 20, 25, ⬜, ⬜

10, 20, ⬜, 40, 50, ⬜, ⬜

2 Round the numbers to the nearest multiple of ten.

⬜ ⟵ 51

35 ⟶ ⬜

19 ⟶ ⬜

Place value and partitioning

1 Partition the numbers into tens and ones. The first one has been done for you.

a   25

__2_ tens   __5_ ones

20 + 5 = 25

b   34

__ tens   __ ones

⬜ + ⬜ = ⬜

c   68

__ tens   __ ones

⬜ + ⬜ = ⬜

d   96

__ tens   __ ones

⬜ + ⬜ = ⬜

2 **a** Kadir thinks of a number. He adds 10. The answer is 41.

What number was he thinking of? ⬜

b Rosi thinks of a number. She subtracts 10. The answer is 76.

What number was she thinking of? ⬜

c Lucia thinks of a number. She adds 1. The answer is 95.

What number was she thinking of? ⬜

3 Compare the amounts using the < and > signs.

a

b

c 5¢ $ 10 $ 10¢ $ 5 $

d

4 Compare the amounts using the < and > signs.

a $2 ☐ $12

b $3 ☐ $30

c 12°C ☐ 2°C

d 29°C ☐ 32°C

5 Complete the sentences to make them true.
Choose measurements from the list.

77 cm   20 cm   35 cm   6 cm   53 cm

a ☐ cm > ☐ cm

b ☐ cm < ☐ cm

c ☐ cm > ☐ cm

d ☐ cm < ☐ cm

6 Write the sets of numbers in order from smallest to biggest.

20, 2, 22, 72, 12   ☐ , ☐ , ☐ , ☐ , ☐

30, 3, 23, 63, 34   ☐ , ☐ , ☐ , ☐ , ☐

Halves and quarters

 Colour in $\frac{1}{2}$ of each shape.

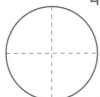 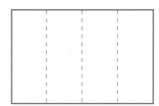

 Colour in $\frac{1}{4}$ of each shape.

  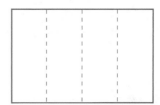

 Colour in $\frac{3}{4}$ of each shape.

  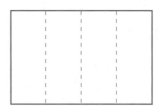

4 Match the equivalent fractions. Draw lines.

 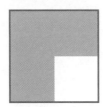

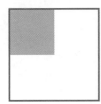 

5 Colour in $\frac{1}{2}$ the objects in each set. Write how many.

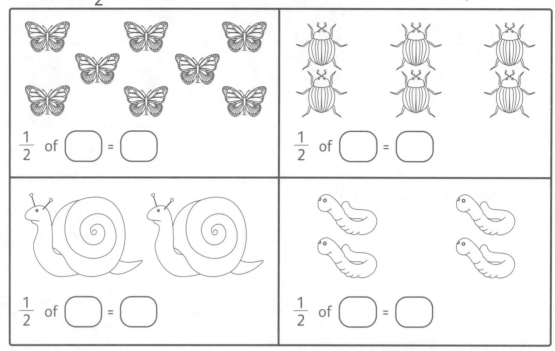

$\frac{1}{2}$ of ◯ = ◯

$\frac{1}{2}$ of ◯ = ◯

$\frac{1}{2}$ of ◯ = ◯

$\frac{1}{2}$ of ◯ = ◯

6 Colour in $\frac{1}{4}$ of the objects in each set. Write how many.

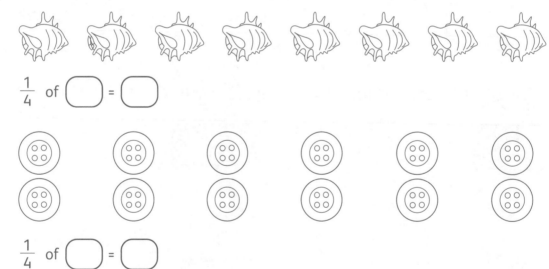

$\frac{1}{4}$ of ◯ = ◯

$\frac{1}{4}$ of ◯ = ◯

7 The baker has 12 eggs. He uses half the eggs.

How many are left? ◯

8 A farmer has 16 goats. He sells $\frac{1}{4}$ of the goats.

How many are left? ◯

Number patterns

1 Use the number line to count in threes.

| 0 | , | 3 | , | 6 | , | | , | | | | |

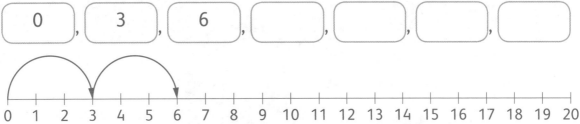

2 Use the number line to count in fours.

| 0 | , | 4 | , | 8 | , | | , | | | | |

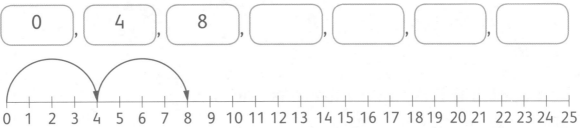

3 Guide the bird across the water to her nest.
Circle the numbers she must follow.
The bird must step on multiples of 5 to miss the hippos.
Each move must be horizontal, vertical or diagonal to the move before. Start on 40.

Self-assessment

Unit 11   Number and problem solving

😃	I understand this well.
😐	I understand this, but I need more practice.
🙁	I don't understand this.

I need more help with …

_____

_____

_____

Self-check statements	😃	😐	🙁
I can partition numbers into tens and ones and know what each digit means.			
I can work out 1 or 10 more or less than any number and explain what happens to the digits.			
I can put a group of numbers to 100 in order.			
I can use the < and > signs to compare numbers.			
I know if a shape is divided into halves or quarters.			
I can show halves and quarters as equivalent fractions.			
I can work out one half and one quarter of a set of objects.			
I can count in twos, fives and tens to help count groups of numbers.			
I can count on in threes and fours using a number line.			
I can recognise if a number is a multiple of 2, 5 or 10.			

Unit 12 Geometry and problem solving

Can you remember?

a Match the shapes to their names.

| hexagon | square | rectangle | circle | pentagon | triangle |

b Complete the table and describe each shape.

Shape	Number of sides and corners
Circle	1 curved side, 0 corners
Triangle	3 sides, 3 corners
Square	
Rectangle	
Pentagon	
Hexagon	

2-D and 3-D shapes

1 Think of an example around you for each shape. Draw a picture.

Shape	Name	Picture
●		
▲		
◼		
◼	rectangle	My Book

2 Colour all the circles. How many circles can you see? [   ]

3 Match the 3-D shape to its face. Some will match more than one face.

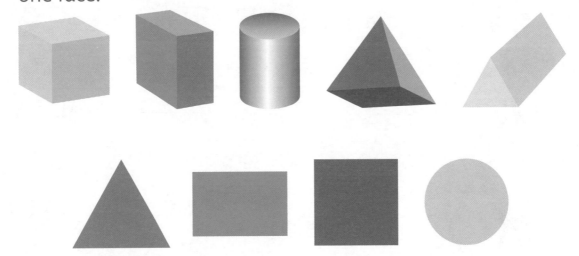

4 Draw a line of symmetry on each shape.

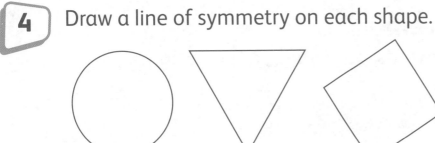

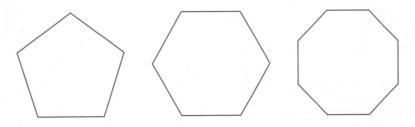

5 Complete the patterns to make them symmetrical.

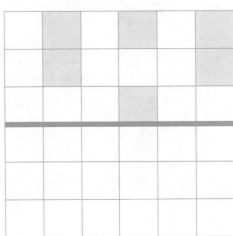

6 Draw a line of symmetry on each pattern.

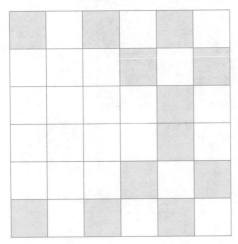

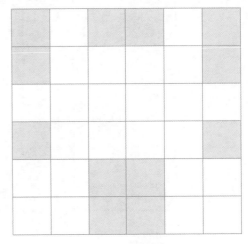

Position and movement

The robot can move forwards, backwards, left and right.

Imagine you are the robot. Which way do you need to go?

Backwards

Right   Left

Forwards

Help the robot move through the maze.
Follow the directions on page 67.

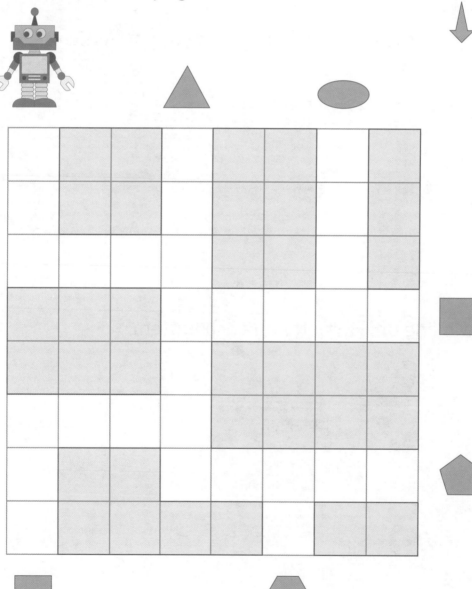

Follow the directions. Which shape does the robot walk to?

a Forwards 3 squares, left turn, forwards 3 squares, right turn, backwards 2 squares.

b Forwards 3 squares, left turn, forwards 3 squares, right turn, forwards 4 squares, left turn, forwards 4 squares.

c Forwards 3 squares, left turn, forwards 3 squares, right turn, forwards 1 square, left turn, forwards 4 squares.

d Forwards 3 squares, left turn, forwards 3 squares, right turn, forwards 3 squares, right turn, forwards 3 squares, left turn, forwards 2 squares.

2 The shape moves a quarter-turn anti-clockwise.
Tick the correct shape in each row.

a

b

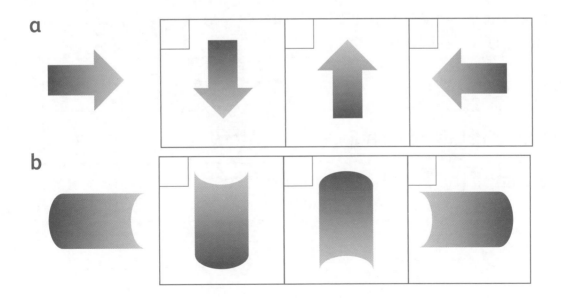

Self-assessment

Unit 12   Geometry and problem solving

😊 I understand this well.

😐 I understand this, but I need more practice.

☹️ I don't understand this.

I need more help with …

_____

_____

_____

Self-check statements	😊	😐	☹️
I can look at pictures of 2-D shapes and name them.			
I can sort sets of 2-D shapes in different ways.			
I can describe different shapes and talk about their properties.			
I can draw a line of symmetry on a shape.			
I can complete a symmetrical picture by drawing the 'other half'.			
I can name 3-D shapes.			
I can find and describe shapes around me.			
I can describe the 2-D shapes on the faces of 3-D shapes.			

Can you remember?

20 + 10 = ☐   20 + 20 = ☐   20 + 30 = ☐

50 + 10 = ☐   50 + 20 = ☐   50 + 30 = ☐

Addition and subtraction

 1 a

20 + 7 = ☐

22 + 7 = ☐

b

30 + 7 = ☐

32 + 7 = ☐

2 a 22 + 27 = ☐   b 45 + 13 = ☐   c 64 + 23 = ☐

32 + 27 = ☐   45 + 23 = ☐   64 + 33 = ☐

3 There are 18 motorbikes and 21 cars on the ferry.

How many vehicles are there altogether? ☐

4 Choose the best method to solve the calculations.
Complete the table.

Find the difference (counting on)	Take away (counting back)
57 – 54 =	82 – 3 =

81 – 78   73 – 69
63 – 60   95 – 91
52 – 49   76 – 12
53 – 8   49 – 7
86 – 5   28 – 23

5 Solve the calculations.

a 89 – 87 = ☐   b 46 – 45 = ☐   c 55 – 4 = ☐

d 78 – 7 = ☐   e 38 – 32 = ☐   f 29 – 4 = ☐

6 There are 67 seats on an aeroplane. Complete the table.

Day	Empty seats	Passengers
Monday	4	
Tuesday	5	
Wednesday		61
Thursday		59

Multiplication and division

 Count in 2s, 5s and 10s to work out the answers.

a

How many wellington boots are there? ☐

b

How many arms do the starfish have altogether? ☐

c

How much money is there? ☐

 a Colour in the multiples of 3.
b Circle the multiples of 4.

1	2	3	4	5	6	7	8	9	10
11	12	13	14	15	16	17	18	19	20
21	22	23	24	25	26	27	28	29	30
31	32	33	34	35	36	37	38	39	40
41	42	43	44	45	46	47	48	49	50
51	52	53	54	55	56	57	58	59	60
61	62	63	64	65	66	67	68	69	70
71	72	73	74	75	76	77	78	79	80
81	82	83	84	85	86	87	88	89	90
91	92	93	94	95	96	97	98	99	100

3 Solve the calculations.

45 ÷ 5 = ⬜   60 ÷ 10 = ⬜   20 ÷ 2 = ⬜

40 ÷ 5 = ⬜   50 ÷ 10 = ⬜   18 ÷ 2 = ⬜

35 ÷ 5 = ⬜   40 ÷ 10 = ⬜   16 ÷ 2 = ⬜

4 Solve the calculations.

15 ÷ 3 = ⬜   15 ÷ 5 = ⬜

16 ÷ 3 = ⬜   16 ÷ 5 = ⬜

17 ÷ 3 = ⬜   17 ÷ 5 = ⬜

Sometimes when we divide, there are some left over.

5 The children had 12 shells. They put 4 shells on each sandcastle.

How many sandcastles are there? ⬜

6 The children had 13 flags. They put 4 flags on each sandcastle.

How many sandcastles are there? ⬜

How many flags are left over? ⬜

7 There are 14 sandwiches at the picnic. There are 4 sandwiches

for each child. How many children are there? ⬜

How many sandwiches are left over? ⬜

8 There are 15 figs at the picnic. There are 4 figs for each child.

How many figs are left over? ⬜

Missing number problems

 There are 20 counters. Carlos hides some under the cup.
How many counters are under the cup?

 Solve the calculations.

$46 - 45 = \boxed{}$ $\boxed{} - 2 = 65$ $63 + \boxed{} = 69$

$\boxed{} + 7 = 99$ $37 - 31 = \boxed{}$ $\boxed{} - 26 = 1$

3 Make up a story for each number sentence.

Example

 $12 + \boxed{} = 20$

Rosi had 12 marbles. She was given more marbles.
She then had 20 marbles.
How many marbles was Rosi given?

a $18 + \boxed{} = 20$

b $30 - \boxed{} = 25$

Self-assessment

Unit 13　Number and problem solving

😊 I understand this well.

😐 I understand this, but I need more practice.

☹️ I don't understand this.

I need more help with …

_____

_____

_____

Self-check statements	😊	😐	☹️
I can add some two-digit numbers and explain my method.			
I can show how to solve word problems using pictures or objects.			
I can find the difference between two near numbers and can explain how to subtract by taking away and by finding the difference.			
I know all the doubles of multiples of 5 up to double 50.			
I can solve problems by counting in twos, fives and tens.			
I can describe patterns of 3× and 4× tables on the 100 square.			
I understand that division can leave some left over.			
I can explain the methods I use to solve problems and solve number sentences with missing numbers.			
I can make up a story for a missing number calculation.			

Unit 14 Measure and problem solving

Can you remember?

Draw the hands on the clock to show half past 9.

Which day comes before Friday? [   ]

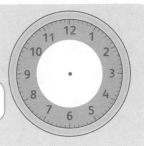

Money

1 Draw a circle around three coins to make each total.

$1.05	
$1.25	
$1.75	

2 Use two notes and three coins to make $20.75.

3 Lemons cost $1 each and oranges cost $1.50 each.

a Mia buys 5 lemons and 2 oranges.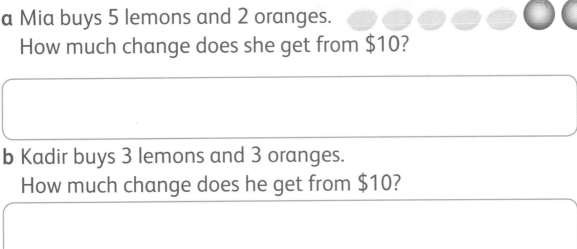
How much change does she get from $10?

b Kadir buys 3 lemons and 3 oranges.
How much change does he get from $10?

75

Measuring capacity

1 Estimate the capacity of these containers. Draw lines to match.

10 ℓ

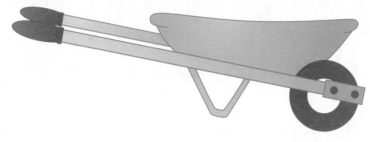

100 ℓ

250 ml

2 ℓ

2 Use <, > or = to compare the amounts.

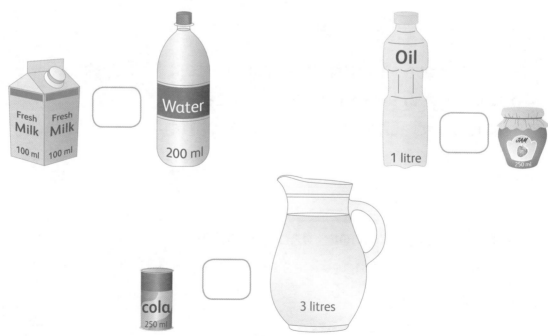

3 How much water is in each measuring jug?

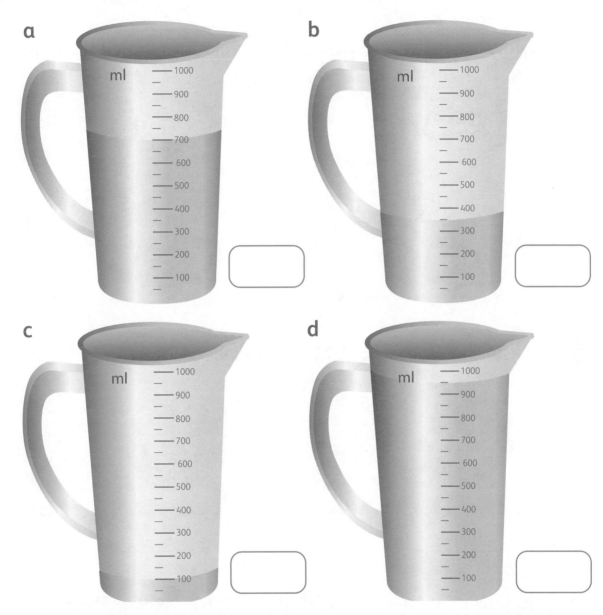

a

b

c

d

4

You will need
a measuring jug and water

a Pour these amounts into the jug.

- 200 ml
- 250 ml
- 450 ml
- 1000 ml

b Will the total amount fill a 2-litre bottle?

Time

1 Draw the hands on each analogue clock to match the digital time.

2 Write the times in order from earliest to latest.

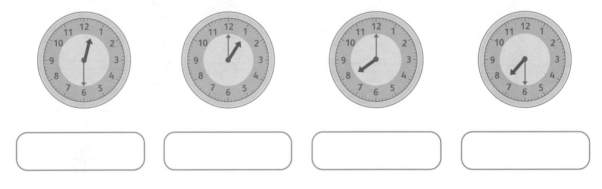

3 Julio went into the dentist at 4 o'clock. He was there for 1 hour. What time did he come out?

4 Mia went into the hairdresser at 1 o'clock. She left at 3 o'clock. How long was she at the hairdresser?

5 Choose the best unit to measure the time of each event. Draw lines to match.

brushing your teeth

seconds

a plane journey

minutes

winking your eye

hours

6 **a** How many days are there in five weeks?

b How many months are there in two years?

Self-assessment

Unit 14 Measure and problem solving

😊	I understand this well.
😐	I understand this, but I need more practice.
☹️	I don't understand this.

I need more help with …

_____

_____

_____

Self-check statements	😊	😐	☹️
I can pay for items with a mix of coins and notes.			
I can work out the change when I pay for an item.			
I can compare the capacity of containers.			
I can use measuring jugs to find the capacity of different containers.			
I can read the time to the half-hour on digital and analogue clocks.			
I know the different units we use to measure time.			
I know how many days there are in a week and how many months there are in a year.			

INTRODUCTION ...

- These student worksheets are designed to act alongside the corresponding revision guide to help reinforce your understanding and improve your confidence.

- Every worksheet is cross-referenced to "The Essentials of G.C.S.E. DESIGN AND TECHNOLOGY: RESISTANT MATERIALS" edited by Brian Russell.

- The questions concentrate purely on the content you need to cover, and the limited space forces you to choose your answer carefully.

These worksheets can be used ...

... as <u>classwork sheets</u> where pupils use their revision guide to provide the answers ...

... as <u>harder classwork sheets</u> where pupils study the topic first, then answer the questions without their guides ...

... as easy to mark <u>homework sheets</u> which test understanding and reinforce learning ...

... as the basis for <u>learning homeworks</u> which are then tested in subsequent lessons ...

... as <u>test material</u> for topics ...

... as a <u>structured revision programme</u> prior to the exams.

- Remember to fill in your score at the bottom of each page in the small grey box, and also to put your score in the 'marks' column on the contents page.

EDITED BY: BRIAN RUSSELL

Head of Design and Technology at Dixon's City Technology College in Bradford. Member of the Royal College of Art Schools Technology Project writing team. Principal moderator for Product Design at GCSE, and a Gatsby Teacher Fellow for Design and Technology.

CONTENTS

Score | Page No.

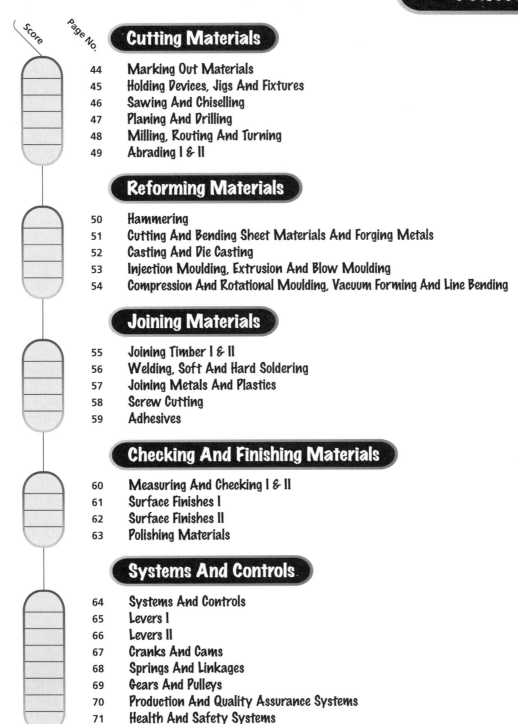

1. a) What is the name of your Awarding Body?

....

b) What is the website address of your Awarding Body?

....

2. What do the initials RMT stand for?

....

3. What makes this course different to other D&T courses?

....

....

....

....

4. Ask your teacher for the following days/dates.

i) Homework night: ....

ii) Mock exam date: .... iii) Year 11 final exam date: ....

5. a) What percentage is your written examination paper worth?

....

b) How long will the examination paper last?

....

6. a) Which THREE types of timber do you need to revise for your written examination?

i) .... ii) .... iii) ....

b) Which THREE types of metal do you need to revise for your written examination?

i) .... ii) .... iii) ....

c) Which TWO types of plastic do you need to revise for your written examination?

i) .... ii) ....

d) Name EIGHT other areas which you need to revise for your written examination.

i) .... ii) .... iii) ....

iv) .... v) .... vi) ....

vii) .... viii) ....

1. a) What percentage does your written coursework contribute to your final mark?

b) How much time are you expected to spend on your coursework?

i) Full course: ....   ii) Short course: ....

2. What information should you include in your design folder?

3. What are you expected to manufacture for your coursework project?

4. What is the purpose of the Principle Moderator?

5. Name EIGHT areas of content which should be included in your design folder.

i) ....

ii) ....

iii) ....

iv) ....

v) ....

vi) ....

vii) ....

viii) ....

6. Why is the quality of your written communication important?

7. Give an example of a 'wider implication' which you could include in your project.

1. a) What would you use a set square for?

....

b) What would you use a protractor for?

....

c) What would you use a fineliner pen for?

....

2. Rearrange the following graphite pencil grades in order of hardness (one has been done for you).

	B	H	3H	2B	HB	
HARD	( )	( )	(HB)	( )	( )	SOFT

3. Which grades of graphite pencil are used for the following?

USE	GRADE
Drawing construction lines:	....
Simple shading and drawing:	....
Quick, freehand sketching:	....

4. Give TWO uses for a camera during this course.

i) .... ii) ....

5. a) What advantage is there in using a circle template?

....

b) What advantage is there in using an ellipse template?

....

6. What advantages are there in using a computer during your course?

....

....

....

....

1. How many A3 sheets should you aim to produce for your project?

2. a) How should you start your project?

b) Why is it useful to work out a time-plan for your project?

3. a) The '4P's method of brainstorming is useful for organising your first thoughts. List the '4P's.

i) .... ii) .... iii) .... iv) ....

b) You are going to design a child's toy box. Complete the table below to show how you will consider the problem and organise your first thoughts using the '4P's method.

Jobs to do:

i) ....

ii) ....

iii) ....

iv) ....

Jobs to do:

i) ....

ii) ....

iii) ....

iv) ....

P ....

P ....

FIRST THOUGHTS FOR A CHILD'S TOY BOX

P ....

P ....

Jobs to do:

i) ....

ii) ....

iii) ....

iv) ....

Jobs to do:

i) ....

ii) ....

iii) ....

iv) ....

1. a) Explain what you mean by the word 'Anthropometrics.'

....

b) Why do designers try to work to the 5th - 95th percentile when it comes to measurements?

....

c) Explain what you mean by the word 'Ergonomics.'

....

2. List FOUR areas which are covered by ergonomics.

i) ....   ii) ....

iii) ....   iv) ....

3. Designers often use ergonomics to assist with the position of key features in a design. Use the ergonome, on a separate A3 sheet, to design TWO of the following:

i) The driving position on a Go-kart

ii) A computer workstation

iii) A mountain bicycle

iv) An office chair

v) A garden lounger

vi) A portable workbench

4. a) Colour is an important ergonomic consideration. Add colour to the two products below ...

i) ... to avoid problems with 'left' and 'right'.

ii) ... to improve the visibility of the lifejacket in the sea.

b) Explain your thinking regarding the colours of the above two products.

....

....

....

....

ANTHROPOMETRIC DATA IS PROVIDED IN THE REVISION GUIDE.

1. a) Measure TWO people and complete the chart below.

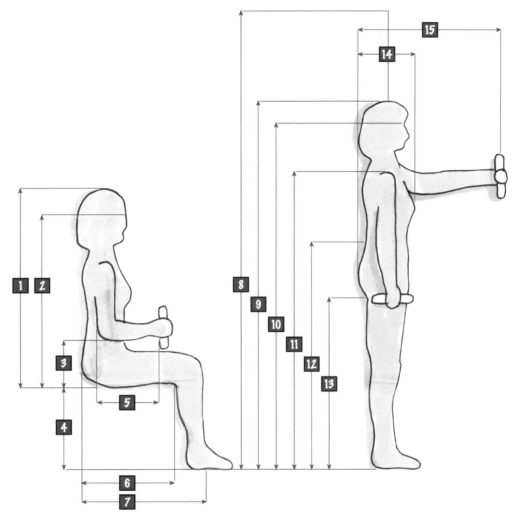

1.	Sitting Height	....	....	8.	Vertical Grip Reach	....	....
2.	Sitting Eye Height	....	....	9.	Stature	....	....
3.	Sitting Elbow Height	....	....	10.	Eye Height	....	....
4.	Popliteal Height	....	....	11.	Shoulder Height	....	....
5.	Elbow-grip Length	....	....	12.	Elbow Height	....	....
6.	Buttock-popliteal Length	....	....	13.	Knuckle Height	....	....
7.	Buttock-knee Length	....	....	14.	Chest Depth	....	....
	Body Weight			15.	Forward Grip Reach	....	....

b) How does the data in the table above compare with the data provided in the Revision Guide?

....
....
....

Choose a product and complete the following:

1. **a)** In the space below, draw the product from TWO different view points.

b) List the main materials used and explain why each was chosen.

MATERIAL	REASON THE MATERIAL WAS USED

c) Who is the product aimed at and what is its main function?

User group:

Main function:

d) Describe ONE ergonomic feature of the product.

e) How was the product manufactured?

f) What other factors should you consider?

1. Describe TWO methods of recording the responses from an interview.

i) ....

ii) ....

2. Questionnaires can provide useful data. List THREE time-effective ways of collecting such data.

i) ....

ii) ....

iii) ....

3. Look at the survey data below and analyse the results.

Favourite Programme	Fireman Sam	Bob the Builder	Tweenies	Telly Tubbies
Number of Children	8 boys, 4 girls	12 boys, 2 girls	6 boys, 6 girls	4 boys, 8 girls

i) What is the total number of children in the survey?

....

ii) What percentage are boys?

....

iii) What is the most popular programme?

....

iv) What percentage of children chose the most popular programme?

....

v) If an equal number of boys and girls had taken part in the survey which programme would you expect to be the most popular? Explain your choice.

....

....

4. You have been asked to design a toy box which has one of the characters from the programmes above on it. Using the data from the survey which one would you choose and why?

....

....

....

1. Name THREE sources from which secondary information on materials can be collected.

   i) ....

   ii) ....

   iii) ....

2. List FIVE tests which could be used on your potential materials.

   i) ....

   ii) ....

   iii) ....

   iv) ....

   v) ....

3. Using sketches and notes, explain in detail how you would conduct your own test to find out the stiffest material which could be used in a frame structure.

1. a) What gains you more credit; primary or secondary research?

b) Give TWO examples of primary research.

i) .... ii) ....

c) Give TWO examples of secondary research.

i) .... ii) ....

2. Choose a commercially manufactured product and write a specification for it which would provide answers to the following questions:

a) What is the product?

b) Who is the target market?

c) What does the product do?

d) Are there any size/weight issues?

e) How long is the product expected to last and are there any maintenance issues?

f) What aesthetic issues are there?

g) What properties do the materials of the product need to have?

h) Are there any other requirements of the product or its packaging?

1. Using any of the techniques as shown on page 20 and 21 of the revision guide, sketch an idea for a piece of fashion jewellery. Add notes to explain the materials and constructions you intend to use.

2. a) Use the grid below to produce ideas for a modular storage/display system which would be suitable for a teenager's bedroom.

b) Why are grids often used when designing furniture?

1. How are the best ideas sheets formed?

2. How do you record any modelling which you may have undertaken at this stage?

3. What annotations are needed on your ideas sheets?

4. Add suitable annotations to the two ideas shown below for a storage box (additional detail drawings might also be required to clarify your annotations).

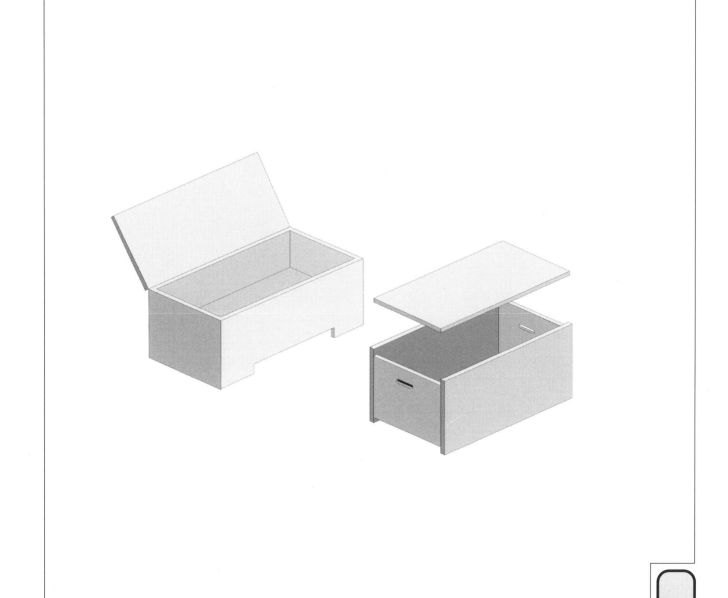

1. a) Re-draw the idea shown below making ONE change only. Re-draw idea 2 making ONE more change.
   Repeat until each box is complete.

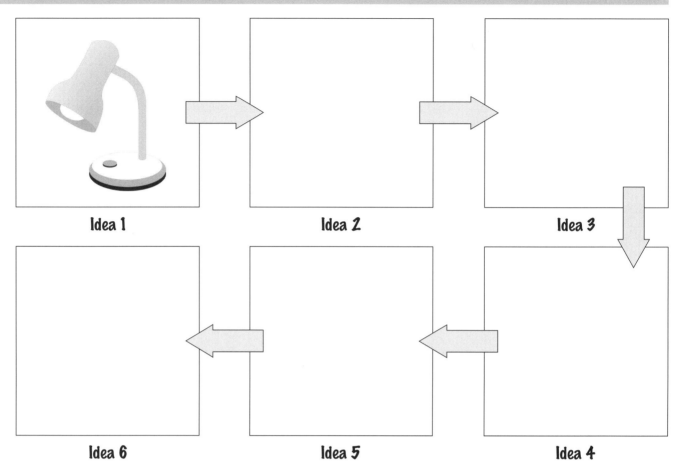

Idea 1   Idea 2   Idea 3

Idea 6   Idea 5   Idea 4

b) For each of the re-drawn ideas above seek other people's opinion.
   Write their comments in the spaces below.

Idea 2: ....
....

Idea 3: ....
....

Idea 4: ....
....

Idea 5: ....
....

Idea 6: ....
....

1. Name THREE suitable materials for making scale models.

i) .... ii) .... iii) ....

2. Describe in detail how you would model each of the two designs shown below.

i) ....
....
....
....
....
....
....
....
....
....
....
....

ii) ....
....
....
....
....
....
....
....
....
....
....
....

3. Give THREE reasons why you might need to model an idea before you start making it.

i) ....
ii) ....
iii) ....

1. Name and explain what each of the following flow chart symbols represent.

i)

ii)

iii)

iv)

i) ....

ii) ....

iii) ....

iv) ....

2. a) Using these symbols draw a flow chart which shows how you could manufacture the box shown. Remember to show where and how the quality checks will be made.

b) When should you include a feedback loop in your flow chart?

....

1. Give TWO advantages of using CAD at the development stage of a project.

i) ....

ii) ....

2. a) Explain the term 'Electronic Product Definition.'

....
....
....

b) Why is Electronic Product Definition used in industry?

....
....
....

3. Using diagrams and notes, explain the term 'nesting.'

....
....
....
....
....
....
....
....

4. What does 'CNC' mean?

....

5. Give TWO ways in which CAD work could be presented in your design folder.

i) ....

ii) ....

6. Give ONE reason why it is important to have at least one CAD drawing in your coursework design folder.

....
....

1. What is a Design Proposal?

2. Why is a presentation drawing often used as part of a design proposal?

3. What is Pro/DESKTOP and why is it so commonly used in D&T?

4. Using a ruler produce a presentation drawing of a simple wooden box. Use colour to make it look like the real materials used.

5. Explain why it is important to have at least ONE presentation drawing in your coursework design folder.

1. Why should evaluation take place at every stage of the design process?

2. What should you include in your final evaluation report?

3. Other people's opinions are a useful starting point for a final evaluation report. List SIX questions which you could ask people.

   i)

   ii)

   iii)

   iv)

   v)

   vi)

4. Why is it important to check your prototype against your specification?

5. You have completed your prototype. What can you do if you feel that your original design specification was faulty?

6. What is the value of explaining any changes made during the making stage of the design process?

7. Is it worth word processing your evaluation report? Explain your answer.

1. a) What is meant by the term 'Field Testing?'

b) Why is non-destructive testing so important?

c) What safety precautions should you take when asking children to test out your prototype?

2. a) Explain how you might seek opinions on your prototype from other experts.

b) Why is it important to comment on other people's thoughts of your prototype?

c) What happens if your prototype is a complete failure?

3. a) There is almost always a need to make modifications to your prototype before your design can go into commercial production. List, in order of priority, the THREE key questions you should ask yourself about your design at this stage.

i)

ii)

iii)

b) Name FOUR manufacturing aids which would ensure that ten or more duplicate prototypes could be produced.

i)   ii)

iii)   iv)

1. Complete the following table:

TYPE OF PRODUCTION	METHOD OF PRODUCTION	TYPICAL PRODUCT
....	Product is continually produced over a period of hours, days or even years.	....
Mass	....	....
....	....	Display for an exhibition stand
'Just in Time'	....	....
....	A series of products, which are all the same are made together in either small or large quantities.	....

2. Suggest a problem which could occur during commercial production of the following:

a) 'One-off' production of a boardroom table.

```
......................................................................
......................................................................
......................................................................
......................................................................
```

b) Mass production of a range of kitchen units.

```
......................................................................
......................................................................
......................................................................
......................................................................
```

c) 'Just in Time' production of a motor car.

```
......................................................................
......................................................................
```

1. Accurately draw a freehand square, circle and equilateral triangle in the space below. Use a ball point pen or fineliner pen.

2. Based on the geometric shapes above, draw a freehand side view design of a new clock and a new lamp.

Clock design

Lamp design

3. Use the 'crating out' method to produce a 3D view of this toy train.

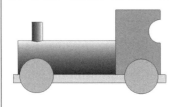

1. Using a 2B or soft graphite pencil, demonstrate your skill in applying tone by shading this box from white to black.

2. Add tone to these shapes to make them appear solid (or three dimensional).

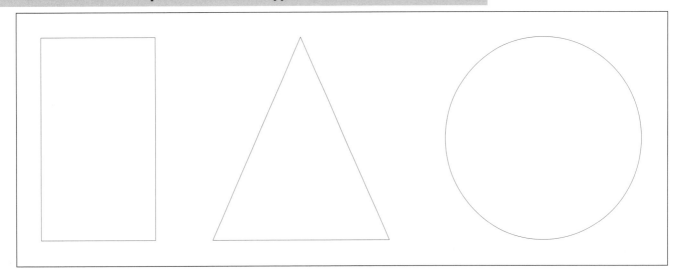

3. Add colour, tone and texture to the objects below to illustrate the materials.

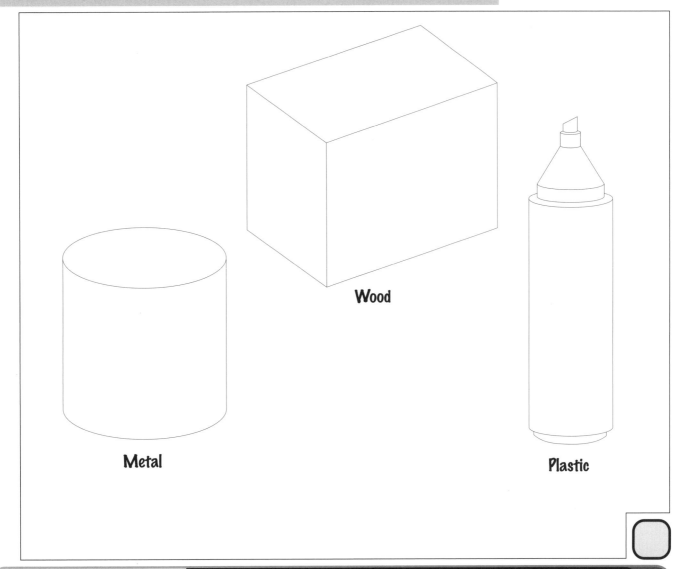

Wood

Metal

Plastic

1. Using isometric projection, draw a cube which is exactly 40mm.

2. Re-draw this unit using isometric projection. You can choose your own measurements to fit it into the space below.

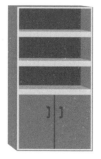

1. Demonstrate your ability to draw circles in isometric by producing your own design for a camera. Use the example for general guidance.

2. Produce an exploded isometric drawing of the train to show how the wheels are attached to the base.

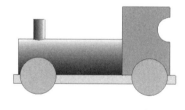

1. Explain the term 'Working Drawing.'

_____

_____

2. The British Standards Institute has set standards for lines on working drawings. Explain the following uses.

i) Continuous thick lines are used for:

_____

ii) Continuous thin lines are used for:

_____

iii) Chain thin lines are used for:

_____

3. The British Standards Institute has set standards for dimensioning on working drawings.

i) What unit of measurement is used? _____

ii) Why is this unit of measurement used? _____

iii) Where are numbers written? _____

4. Dimension the drawing below to BSI standards.

5. What does the following symbol mean?

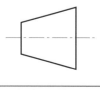

_____

_____

1. What is the purpose of 3rd Angle Orthographic Projection?

....
....
....

2. Use 3rd Angle Orthographic Projection to produce a full-size drawing of a tape cassette.
   Add main dimensions and show the scale.

1. Give TWO reasons for using ICT in your coursework.

i) ....

ii) ....

2. Explain how you might use the following ICT applications in your coursework.

i) Word Processing Packages: ....

....

ii) Spreadsheets: ....

....

iii) DeskTop Publishing Software: ....

....

3. Explain in detail how you might use the following in your coursework.

i) Digital Camera: ....

....

....

ii) Scanner: ....

....

iii) Graphics Packages: ....

....

iv) Plotter/Cutter: ....

....

....

v) The Internet: ....

....

vi) CD Roms: ....

....

vii) CAD Packages: ....

....

viii) 3D Modelling Packages: ....

....

1. What is the difference between CAD and CAM?

....
....
....

2. What is 'Post Processing?'

....
....
....

3. a) What is the difference between a two-axis machine and a three-axis machine?

....
....
....

b) Complete the table to show whether the following machines are two-axis or three-axis.

| PLOTTERS | ROUTERS | LATHES | VINYL CUTTERS | MILLING MACHINES | ENGRAVING MACHINES |

TWO-AXIS MACHINES	THREE-AXIS MACHINES

4. a) What is the difference between a three-axis machine and a four-axis machine?

....
....
....

b) Why is it very rare for a school to have a four-axis machine?

....
....
....

5. a) What is 'Rapid Prototyping?'

....
....
....

b) How might you be able to recreate something 'similar' at school?

....
....

1. Below are the three main types of timber and a list of descriptions. Match the type of timber to the correct description with an arrow.

HARDWOODS	Come from coniferous trees.
	Made by gluing wood layers or wood fibres together.
SOFTWOODS	An example of this type of timber is balsa.
	Developed mainly for industrial production techniques.
MANUFACTURED BOARDS	Generally grow faster than hardwoods.
	Generally harder than softwoods.
	Can be produced in very long sheets with a consistent quality.
	Come from deciduous or broad-leafed trees.

2. Name SIX types of manufactured board.

i) ....   ii) ....

iii) ....   iv) ....

v) ....   vi) ....

3. Different timbers have different characteristics which need to be considered when choosing a particular timber for a specific purpose. Explain the following characteristics.

i) Workability: ....

....

ii) Colour: ....

....

iii) Structural Strength: ....

....

iv) Grain Pattern: ....

....

v) Texture: ....

....

4. Which are more environmentally friendly, hardwoods or softwoods? Explain your choice.

....

....

1. Complete the following table:

HARDWOOD	TYPICAL PROPERTIES	USES
....	....	To make casting patterns
Mahogany	....	....
....	Resistant to moisture	....
....	....	To make hammer handles
Beech	....	....
....	Open grained, difficult to work	....

2. Choose a suitable hardwood, and explain your choice, for the following projects.

a) A school laboratory is being re-fitted with timber tables.

b) A traditional cottage is being renovated and new beams are required.

c) A toy manufacturer is producing wooden trains.

d) A boat is being built.

e) A furniture manufacturer is producing a wooden garden bench.

3. Thin layers of hardwood are often glued onto manufactured boards such as MDF.

a) What is the name given to this technique?

b) Give TWO reasons why this is done.

i) ....

ii) ....

1. Below are TEN statements which describe properties of five different softwoods.
Using coloured pencils link each property to the correct softwood.

Creamy-yellow	Cream/Pale Brown	Reddish Brown	Pale Yellow	Pale Yellow with Red/Brown streaks

Yellow Cedar	Parana Pine	Spruce	Scots Pine	Western Red Cedar

Not very durable	Light in weight but stiff and stable	Fairly strong and inexpensive	Easy to work with but weak and expensive	Fairly strong, durable and expensive

2. Choose a suitable softwood, and explain your choice, for the following projects.

    a) A general framework is needed to support a plywood sheet.

    b) A dog kennel is being clad.

    c) A wooden bi-plane is being restored.

    d) Doors and fittings are needed for a new house.

3. You visit your local DIY shop to purchase some softwood.
Which softwood would you expect to be on sale? Explain your reasons.

1. Are the following statements true or false?

i) Plywood is made from chips of wood glued together. ....

ii) Hardboard is a very inexpensive particle board. ....

iii) MDF is easily machined and can be painted or stained. ....

iv) Chipboard is usually veneered or covered in plastic laminate. ....

v) Blockboard has a central layer made from strips of timber. ....

vi) MDF is not available in water and fire-resistant forms. ....

vii) Plywood is constructed from layers of veneer or plies. ....

viii) Chipboard has a central layer made from strips of timber. ....

2. Give TWO reasons why manufactured boards are often used in commercial furniture production.

i) ....

ii) ....

3. Choose a suitable manufactured board, and explain your choice, for the following projects.

a) A school library is being re-fitted with timber shelves.

b) A reproduction panelled room is being created using panels which can be machined.

c) A toy manufacturer is producing a wooden skateboard.

4. A kitchen manufacturer is producing a new range which will be more durable than the previous chipboard model. Name a suitable board and explain your choice.

5. What does the abbreviation WBP found on plywood mean?

1. Below are the three main categories of metal and a list of descriptions. Match the metal to the correct description with an arrow.

FERROUS METALS

NON-FERROUS METALS

ALLOYS

Contain no iron at all.

Substances which contain two or more metals.

Consist mainly of iron.

Copper and aluminium are typical examples.

Can be picked up by a magnet.

Brass is a typical example.

2. a) Where do metals originate from?

   b) What is the corrosion associated with ferrous metals commonly called?

3. Give THREE differences between ferrous metals and non-ferrous metals.

   i)

   ii)

   iii)

4. How is it possible to produce alloys that have specific properties?

5. Different metals have different properties which need to be considered when deciding which metal to use for a specific purpose. Explain the following properties.

   i) Brittleness:

   ii) Tensile Strength:

   iii) Elasticity:

   iv) Work Hardness:

   v) Compressive Strength:

   vi) Ductility:

   vii) Hardness:

   viii) Toughness:

   ix) Malleability:

1. Complete the following table:

FERROUS METAL	TYPICAL PROPERTIES	USE
Cast Iron		
	15% carbon content	
		Drill bits
	Ductile and malleable	
		Kitchen sinks

2. Choose a suitable ferrous metal, and explain your choice, for the following projects.

a) A general framework is needed to support a wooden bench top.

b) Prongs are needed for a new design of garden rake.

c) A Victorian house is being restored and a replacement drain cover is needed.

d) An interior decorator wants to create a 'catering kitchen' look.

3. Why is high speed steel a suitable metal for the construction of drill bits?

4. a) Ferrous metals are often vulnerable to corrosion. What is the most common cause of this corrosion.

b) Give TWO ways in which this corrosion can be prevented.

i)

ii)

1. Below are TEN statements which describe properties of five different non-ferrous metals. Using coloured pencils link each property to the correct non-ferrous metal.

Can be polished to a mirror-like appearance	High resistance to corrosion	Excellent conductor of heat and electricity	Ductile and resistant to corrosion	Extremely resistant to corrosion from moisture

Tin	Lead	Aluminium	Zinc	Copper

Very weak metal	Light in weight	Bright silver in appearance	Reddish-brown metal which is ductile and malleable	Heavy metal with a blue-grey surface

2. Choose a suitable non-ferrous metal, and explain your choice, for the following projects.

   a) A portable camping chair is being produced.

   b) A covering for the top of a pub table is needed.

   c) A Victorian house is being restored and roof flashing is needed.

   d) An interior designer wants punched metal plates to give a kitchen cupboard a French appearance.

3. Why is copper a suitable metal for water pipes?

1. Are the following statements true or false?

i) Casting alloy is mainly aluminium with 3% copper and 5% silicon. ....

ii) Brass is a mixture of copper and tin. ....

iii) Guilding metal is an alloy of copper and zinc. ....

iv) Duralumin is almost as strong as steel. ....

v) Brass is a mixture of 35% copper and 65% zinc. ....

vi) Pewter is mainly tin with a small amount of antimony and copper. ....

vii) Duralumin is an alloy which contains tin. ....

2. a) A lightweight car body is being built. Name a suitable alloy and explain your choice.

b) You have designed a handle which needs sand-casting in the school workshop. Which alloy would you choose and why?

c) A Victorian house is being restored and a replacement door knocker is needed. Name a suitable alloy and explain your choice.

d) A builder wants a decorative metal panel for the front of a shopping mall. Which alloy should the builder use and why?

e) Why is brass a suitable alloy for making a garden tap?

3. a) Modern pewter is now lead-free. Explain why this is a more suitable alloy for making drinking tankards than the older lead-based pewter.

b) Many alloys corrode/discolour when exposed to the atmosphere. Suggest ONE treatment which can preserve their appearance.

1. a) Why have plastics taken over as the most widely used materials in commercial production?

b) Explain the term 'natural' plastics.

c) Explain the term 'synthetic' plastics.

d) i) What is the name of the process of manufacture of synthetic plastics?

ii) Explain the process, using diagrams to help you.

2. a) There are TWO different types of plastic. Name them.

i) ii)

b) For the plastic named in part a) i) above explain how the 'particles' in this plastic are arranged, using a diagram to help you.

c) For the plastic named in part a) ii) above explain how the 'particles' in this plastic are arranged, using a diagram to help you.

d) What happens if each of the plastics above are 'heated up'?

1. Complete the following table:

THERMOPLASTIC	DESCRIPTION	USE
		Blister packaging
	Flexible, can be used as a hinge	
		Gear wheels in child's toy
Polythene, HDPE		
	Glass-like transparency	
High Impact Polystyrene		
		Carrier bags

2. a) A fishing box with a hinged lid is to be manufactured. Name a suitable thermoplastic and explain your choice.

b) You have designed a cover for an alarm to be made in school. Name a suitable thermoplastic and explain your choice.

c) A flexible bottle is needed to hold motor oil. Name a suitable thermoplastic and explain your choice.

d) A designer wants an illuminated sign on a shop front. Name a suitable thermoplastic and explain your choice.

3. Give TWO commercial production methods used for manufacturing products from thermoplastics.

i)   ii)

4. How would you change the property of PVC to create a softer more rubbery material?

1. Complete the following table:

THERMOSETTING PLASTIC	DESCRIPTION	USE
....	....	Boat building
....	Heat resistant	....
....	....	Modern electrical switches
Epoxy Resin	....	....
....	Hard, dark and brittle	....

2. a) Name a suitable thermosetting plastic from which a garden seat could be made at school. Explain your choice.

   b) A wooden kitchen worktop is to be replaced. The new worktop needs to have a finish which is resistant to both water and heat. Name a suitable thermosetting plastic and explain your choice.

   c) Why is melamine formaldehyde a suitable plastic to use when manufacturing plastic crockery?

   d) i) Name a suitable thermosetting plastic for the manufacture of saucepan handles.

      ii) Why is this plastic only suitable for the manufacture of the handle of the saucepan?

      iii) What disadvantage is there in using this plastic?

3. GRP is a composite material which uses a thermosetting plastic resin and glass fibres.
   a) Why is GRP a useful material?

   b) Give ONE disadvantage for the commercial manufacturing of GRP.

1. a) What happens to a smart wire when an electric current passes through it?

    ....

    b) What subsequently happens when the electric current is switched off?

    ....

    c) Give ONE use for a smart wire.

    ....

2. What unusual characteristic does a lenticular polypropylene sheet have?

    ....

3. How can nichrome wire be used for cutting expanded polystyrene?

    ....

4. a) What is a thermocolour sheet?

    ....

    b) What happens if the temperature goes above 27°C?

    ....

    c) Explain how you could use a thermocolour sheet as a temperature indicator for a product you have designed.

    ....

5. Explain how smart colours could be used in the design of a child's toy.

    ....

6. Why is polymorph such a useful material?

    ....

7. Is smart grease as clever as its name suggests? Explain your answer.

    ....

1. a) Name the following tools.

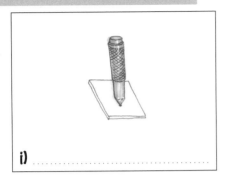

i) ....

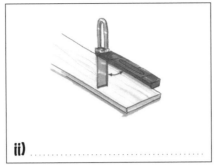

ii) ....

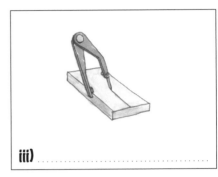

iii) ....

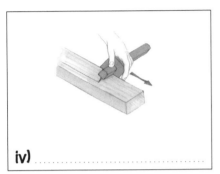

iv) ....

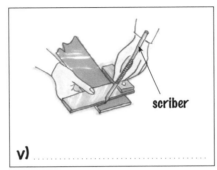

scriber

v) ....

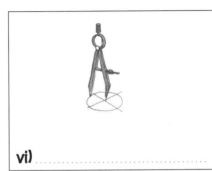

vi) ....

b) Which of the above tools ...

i)   ... is used for scribing lines parallel to a straight edge of timber? ....

ii) ... is used to mark lines at 90° from the edge of a material? ....

iii) ... is used to mark the centre of a hole for drilling into metal? ....

iv) ... is used to mark out circles or arcs? ....

v) ... is used for marking out lines at any angle? ....

2. Card templates are often used for marking out curved shapes on to any material. Explain, using diagrams, how you would use a card template to mark out a symmetrical heart shape.

3. Show how you would mark out two 6mm holes, centrally and 10mm from each end of this material.

1. Name the following holding devices.

i) ....

ii) ....

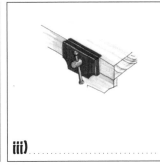

iii) ....

iv) ....

v) ....

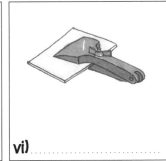

vi) ....

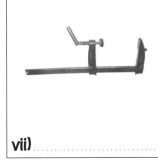

vii) ....

viii) ....

b) Which of the above devices ...

i) ... is excellent for holding wooden joints together whilst gluing? ....

ii) ... is used to hold timber and plastics to the workbench? ....

iii) ... is used for holding a material which is being drilled or milled? ....

iv) ... is used for holding materials at right angles whilst joining together? ....

c) What is the toggle clamp used for?

....
....
....

2. Suggest TWO ways in which a jig can be used to aid production of other products.

i) ....

ii) ....

3. Fixtures are production aids which are attached to machines. Design a fixture which will allow 5mm holes to be drilled every 200mm along a strip of 10mm wide plastic.

1. a) How many teeth should there be in contact with a material when sawing?

   b) Name a saw where the blade is held in tension within a frame.

   c) Name a saw where the blade is fixed directly to the handle.

2. Below are the names of five power saws and a simple description of how they work.
   Match each power saw to the correct description.

Powered Hacksaw	Saw blade is rotated as material is moved across the blade.
Scroll Saw	A forwards/backwards motion of the blade which copies the manual version.
Circular Saw	A continuous strip of saw blade is rotated.
Jigsaw	A reciprocating motion with the blade held in tension.
Bandsaw	A reciprocating motion where the blade is pushed through the material.

3. Explain how you would cut the shape below from sheet timber.

4. Name the following chisels:

   i) ....

   ii) ....

   iii) ....

   iv) ....

5. Name the THREE basic chiselling actions.

   i) ....   ii) ....   iii) ....

6. Explain how a cold chisel works and how it cuts other metals without breaking.

1. Explain what a planing action is.

2. a) Name the following planes.

i) ....

ii) ....

iii) ....

iv) ....

v) ....

b) Which of the above planes would be used for curved surfaces?

3. Explain, using a diagram, how a powered plane works.

4. a) In which direction do all drill bits rotate when cutting?

b) What are drill bits usually made from?

c) What are tungsten-tipped bits used for?

d) How can you tell that a drill bit is designed for a carpenter's brace?

e) If you wanted to drill a hole like the one shown, what drill bit would you use?

f) What is the purpose for using a countersink bit?

g) What is the difference between a power drill and a pedestal drill?

MILLING, ROUTING AND TURNING

1. a) In what way is the process of milling and routing the same?

b) In what way is milling and routing different?

2. a) Name the process being shown in the diagram.

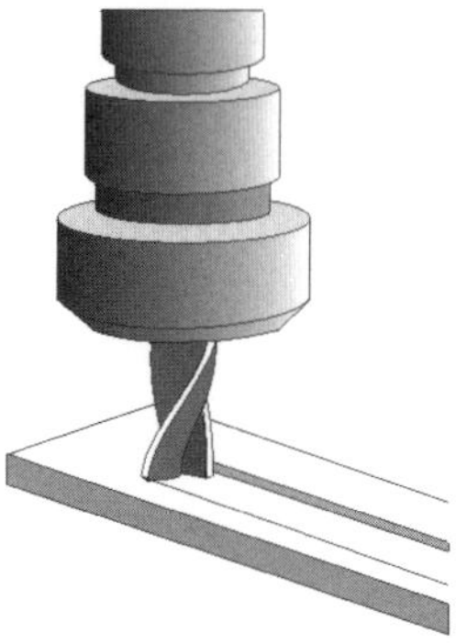

b) On the diagram show the direction of rotation of the cutter.

c) On the diagram show the direction of movement of the table.

3. Explain, using a diagram, what the x, y and z axis do in a milling machine.

4. Explain, very simply, the process involved in CNC milling.

5. a) Explain the process involved in turning.

b) How does a centre lathe work?

c) In what ways is a wood-turning lathe different to a centre lathe?

d) What would be the main advantage of using a CNC lathe?

1. a) Name FOUR abrasive materials which are glued onto a paper or cloth backing.

i) .... ii) ....

iii) .... iv) ....

b) Each sheet of abrasive paper/cloth has a number printed on its back. What does the number mean?

c) What is the function of water when used with 'wet and dry paper'?

d) Why is a cork block used with abrasive paper?

2. a) How do files work?

b) Draw and label the cross-section of five common files.

3. a) Power sanders create several safety hazards. Name TWO and explain what can be done to reduce the risk to Health and Safety.

i) ....

ii) ....

b) Disk sanders can be more difficult to use if accurate angles are required. Explain why.

c) Hand-held power sanders create additional safety hazards. Name TWO and explain what can be done to reduce the risk to Health and Safety.

i) ....

ii) ....

d) Use a coloured pen to mark the edges of this toy animal which can be sanded on a belt sander.

1. Name the following hammers.

i) ....

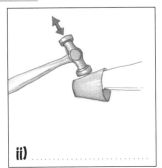

ii) ....

iii) ....

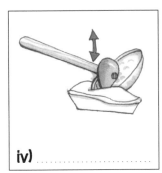

iv) ....

v) ....

vi) ....

vii) ....

b) Which of the above hammers is used ...

i) ... in conjunction with a leather sandbag for hollowing sheet metal? ....

ii) ... for rounding rivets and other pieces of metal? ....

iii) ... for driving chisels and gouges? ....

iv) ... to remove bent nails? ....

v) ... in conjunction with a polished stake for finishing beaten metalwork? ....

vi) ... to start small nails and pins which are held between the fingers? ....

vii) ... for assembling wood joints as well as bending over sheet metals? ....

2. a) Why wouldn't you use a mallet to drive nails through timber?

....

....

....

b) Why wouldn't a claw hammer be the best choice for starting small nails and pins which are held between the fingers?

....

....

....

c) Why wouldn't you use a planishing hammer for general hammering?

....

....

1. a) What are tinsnips used for?

b) Name TWO other shears.

2. What is a folding bar used for?

3. a) In the space provided, draw and label what the punch and die might look like on an industrial press being used to produce toy car bodies.

b) What is used to create the massive pressures needed in industrial presses?

c) Why is sheet metal stamped and pressed cold?

4. a) Explain, briefly, the process of forging.

b) What would a blacksmith use a hearth and anvil for?

c) What is drop forging?

d) What is the name given to the cold forging process used to stamp out coins and metals?

5. Which of the products below are likely to have been forged?

1. a) Briefly describe the process of casting.

b) Name THREE metals which can be formed using sand casting.

i) .... ii) .... iii) ....

c) Patterns are used to create the space in sand casting. What are the patterns made from?

.... or ....

d) Label the parts of this split pattern sand casting set up.

e) In what ways does lost pattern casting differ from split pattern sand casting?

2. a) Name THREE metal alloys suitable for die casting.

i) .... ii) .... iii) ....

b) How are the moulds made for industrial die casting?

c) Explain, using a diagram, how industrial die casting is carried out.

d) Die casting can be carried out in school using basic tools and equipment.
   i) What material would make a suitable mould?

   ii) How could the mould cavity be created?

1. a) Name FOUR materials which are suitable for injection moulding.

i) .... ii) ....

iii) .... iv) ....

b) Explain, briefly, the process involved in injection moulding.

2. a) Name FOUR materials which can be used in the extrusion process.

i) .... ii) ....

iii) .... iv) ....

b) Explain the extrusion process, using a diagram to help you.

3. a) Name THREE materials which are suitable for blow moulding.

i) .... ii) .... iii) ....

b) Explain the ways in which the process of blow moulding is different to extrusion.

c) Another method of blow moulding uses an injection-moulded bottle blank called a parison.

i) Explain simply how this process works.

ii) Why is this process commonly used for making drinks bottles?

1. a) THREE materials are used in compression moulding. Name them.

   i) .... ii) .... iii) ....

   b) Explain the process of compression moulding. Use one suitable diagram to help you.

2. a) Give ONE reason why rotational moulding is a cheaper alternative to injection moulding or blow moulding.

   b) In rotational moulding, why are the mouldings made from polythene?

   c) Name THREE products which can be made using rotational moulding.

   i) .... ii) .... iii) ....

3. a) The diagram shows the process of making products using vacuum forming. Why is the plastic initially heated up?

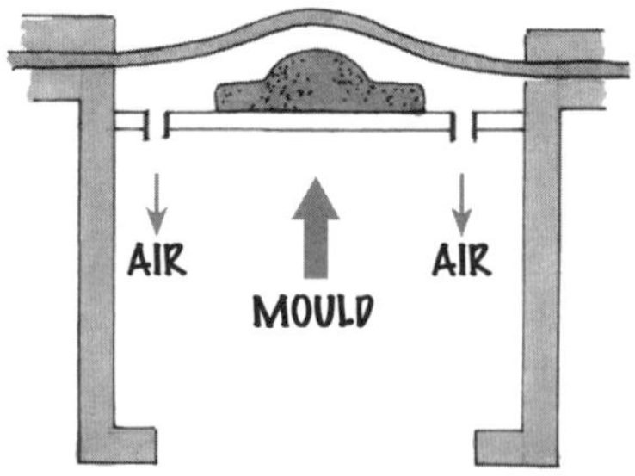

   b) Why is the air 'sucked out'?

   AIR ↑ AIR
   MOULD

   c) What happens as the temperature of the plastic falls?

   d) How is the product separated from the mould?

4. What is line bending?

1. **a) Name the following joints.**

i) ....

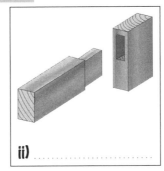
ii) ....

iii) ....

iv) ....

v) ....

vi) ....

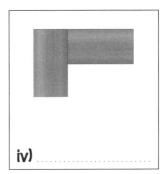
vii) ....

b) Explain how you would mark and cut a halving joint.

2. **a) Give TWO reasons why traditional joints are being replaced in commercial production.**

i) .... ii) ....

b) Nails can be used for making joints.

i) What is the disadvantage of using nails?

ii) How can this disadvantage be overcome?

c) Explain why cross-head screws are replacing traditional screws for the making of joints.

3. **a) What does 'KD' mean?**

b) Draw and label TWO different KD fittings.

1. What are the THREE most common methods of joining metals together using heat and a bonding alloy?

i) .... ii) .... iii) ....

2. a) What should be the most appropriate method of soldering copper plumbing pipes?

....
....

b) Explain the brazing process.

....
....
....
....
....
....
....

c) What is the difference between silver soldering and brazing?

....
....
....
....

3. Name THREE different types of welding.

i) ....
ii) ....
iii) ....

4. Safety is a high priority when welding. Suggest THREE safety precautions you would take.

i) ....
ii) ....
iii) ....

5. Name TWO forms of resistance welding.

i) .... ii) ....

6. Explain how robots can be used to weld metals in commercial production.

....
....
....
....

1. Explain the benefits of mechanical joining over thermal joining.

2. What is the difference between a bolt and a machine screw?

3. Bolts and machine screws are available with many different heads. Draw FOUR alternatives in the spaces below.

4. Suggest FOUR ways in which a nut and bolt/machine screw might be tightened.

Method 1:

Method 2:

Method 3:

Method 4:

5. a) Give ONE advantage and ONE disadvantage for using a rivet to join two materials together compared to using a nut and bolt.

Advantage:

Disadvantage:

b) What are rivets mainly made from?

c) Explain the difference between a traditional rivet and a pop rivet.

1. Explain, using a labelled diagram, how an internal thread can be cut by hand.

2. Explain, using a labelled diagram, how an external thread can be cut by hand.

3. Industrially, threads can be made using a variety of methods. Name THREE.

i) ....

ii) ....

iii) ....

4. Why are most screw cutting taps tapered?

....
....

1. Complete the following table to name suitable adhesives for the joining together of two materials.

	PLASTIC	FABRIC	METAL	WOOD
WOOD				
METAL				
PLASTIC				
FABRIC				

2. a) Describe an appropriate use for a hot melt glue gun.

b) How does solvent cement work?

c) How does epoxy resin work?

d) How does PVA adhesive work?

e) What safety precautions would you need to take if you were using solvent or contact adhesives?

f) Why is it important that any synthetic resin adhesive is not washed down the sink?

3. Choose a suitable adhesive and explain your choice for the following projects.

a) A plastic laminate is bonded to an MDF worktop.

b) A cast pewter motif is glued to the lid of a jewellery box.

c) A display case is made by gluing acrylic together.

d) Beading is glued to an interior softwood door.

1. What tool would you use to measure each of the following lengths?

i) 250mm: .... ii) 25.5mm: .... iii) 2550mm: ....

2. a) What is the disadvantage of using calipers for measuring the outside or inside dimensions of a circular hollow tube?

....

b) Which tool would you use for measuring the inside dimensions of a hollow circular tube?

....

c) Which tool would you use for measuring the outside dimensions of a circular tube?

....

3. When making a cutting list you need to take account of the material thicknesses. Complete the cutting list below in order to make a 300mm cube from 12mm MDF.

DESCRIPTION	NO. OF	LENGTH	WIDTH	THICKNESS	MATERIAL
Sides				12mm	MDF
Top				12mm	MDF
Base				12mm	MDF

4. What is a spirit level used for? ....

5. a) Explain how measuring checks might form part of a quality assurance procedure.

....

b) In what way are the following tools used as checking devices?

i) Measuring Stick: ....

ii) Gap Gauge: ....

iii) Try Square: ....

6. Industrial measuring and checking relies on much more sophisticated technologies. Name TWO methods used.

i) .... ii) ....

1. a) What are the THREE main groups of paints?

> i) ....
>
> ii) ....
>
> iii) ....

b) For the following applications name a suitable paint.

> i) Spraying a metal chair: ....
>
> ii) Brushing onto a wall: ....
>
> iii) Roller painting a toy box made from MDF: ....

2. What is the purpose of primer?

> ....

3. Name THREE different finishes available in varnishes. For each finish suggest a use.

> i) .... Use: ....
>
> ii) .... Use: ....
>
> iii) .... Use: ....

4. Give ONE advantage of a hammered finish paint.

>

5. Give TWO reasons for applying a surface finish.

> i) ....
>
> ii) ....

6. Give TWO Health and Safety risks associated with using solvent-based finishes.

> i) .... ii) ....

7. What is used to clean brushes which have been used with oil-based paints?

> ....

8. Oil can be used as a surface finish. Give TWO examples and a suitable use for each oil.

> Oil: .... Use: ....
>
> Oil: .... Use: ....

1. a) What are wood stains used for?

b) What is needed on top of a wood stain to prevent moisture penetration?

2. Explain the purpose of sanding sealer.

3. a) Explain the THREE stages involved in the process of plastic dip-coating.

b) Explain why powder coating is a more sophisticated version of dip-coating.

4. a) Which TWO surface finishes involve electrolysis?

i) .... ii) ....

b) Which of the above is the common finishing process used on aluminium?

c) What is the disadvantage of using the other surface finish?

5. a) What is the disadvantage of galvanising?

b) What is the advantage of galvanising?

6. Explain the term 'self-finishing.'

1. a) Name TWO methods of polishing timber.

   i) ....

   ii) ....

   b) Explain how wax polish works on timber.

   ....

   c) Name TWO different types of polish used on timber.

   i) .... ii) ....

2. a) Why are metal polishes slightly abrasive?

   ....

   ....

   b) Name a very common metal polish which is found in many households.

   ....

3. a) Name an example of a hard plastic which can be polished.

   ....

   b) What is the purpose of using a metal polish on a plastic?

   ....

   c) Plastics are often polished on their cut edges. Explain why.

   ....

   d) The diagram below shows a buffing wheel being used to polish plastic.
      i) What is the purpose of using a polishing compound such as Vonax?

   ....

   ii) What would happen if the plastic was pressed too hard onto the
       buffing wheel?

   ....

   ....

   ....

1. What THREE parts make up a system?

2. This jigsaw uses a mechanical system. Describe the input and the output.

Input: ....

Output: ....

3. Commercial production can be described as a series of systems. What would be ...

i) ... the Input? ....

ii) ... the Output? ....

4. List THREE areas of commercial production which require organising into sub-systems.

i) ....

ii) ....

iii) ....

5. Briefly discuss the following statement:
'Any manufacturing system is only as good as its Quality Assurance procedures.'

6. a) Health and Safety systems deal with every stage of a product's life. Complete the chart below.

M ....

U ....

D ....

b) Why is feedback essential for any Health and Safety system that deals with any stage of a product's life?

1. Using arrows to clarify your answer, explain the following movements:

i) Rotating Movement: ....

ii) Linear Movement: ....

iii) Reciprocating Movement: ....

iv) Oscillating Movement: ....

2. Explain the following terms associated with levers.

i) Effort: ....

ii) Fulcrum: ....

iii) Load: ....

3. a) This pair of scissors is being used to cut paper.
   i) Label the fulcrum.

   ii) Show, using arrows to indicate movement, where the effort force and load force are applied.

   b) What would happen to the effort force if the scissors were being used to cut thicker paper and why.

....

   c) For the following mechanical toy:
   i) Label the fulcrum.
   ii) Show, using arrows to indicate movement, where the effort force and load force are applied.

1. a) Levers can be used as force multipliers. Explain what this means.

b) Which one of the following levers is acting as a force multiplier? Explain your choice.

A EFFORT   LOAD   B EFFORT   LOAD   C EFFORT   LOAD

F   F   F

c) In the space below accurately draw a simple force multiplier lever where:

i) An effort of 1 could move a load of 2.

ii) An effort of 2 could move a load of 3.

d) For the following force multipliers label the fulcrum and show, using arrows to indicate movement, where the effort force and load force are applied.

i)

ii)

2. a) Explain very simply how a lever can be used as a movement multiplier. Use a diagram to help you.

b) For the following force multipliers label the fulcrum and show, using arrows to indicate movement, where the effort force and load force are applied.

i)

ii)

1. What do cranks and cams convert?

....

2. a) The diagram shows a cam mechanism.

i) Name parts A and B.

A: ....

B: ....

ii) Complete the following sentence:

The cam mechanism shown converts .... motion

into .... motion.

A

B

b) Accurately complete the following diagrams to show how part A of the cam mechanism above would look at each rotating position of part B. For each diagram add arrows to show the movement of part A and B.

i)	ii)	iii)	iv)	v)

3. The diagrams show a piston and camshaft from a car. Explain using sketches and notes how they work together to achieve rotary motion.

....

....

....

....

....

1. a) Springs are used in a variety of ways to resist different forces. What do the following springs resist?

i) ....

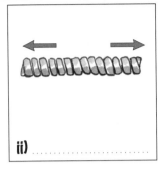

ii) ....

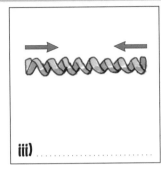

iii) ....

iv) ....

b) How do the springs above resist the forces acting on them?

2. a) What does a linkage transfer?

b) Apart from a tool box name TWO other devices/products which include a linkage.

i) .... ii) ....

c) Explain, using arrows to show direction of movement, how these two linkages work.

i)

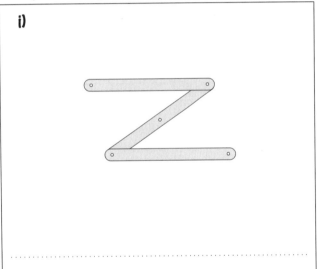

ii)

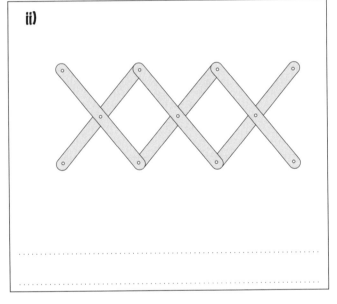

d) Name the TWO linkages shown above.

i) .... ii) ....

3. Draw diagrams to show how you would add a spring to each of the above linkages to ensure that each linkage returns to its original position.

1. a) The diagram shows a spur gear mechanism. On the diagram use an arrow to show the direction of rotation of the small gear if the large gear turns clockwise.

b) How many teeth does the large gear have in relation to the small gear?

c) How many turns will the small gear make when the large gear revolves twice?

2. Name the mechanism shown in the diagram and explain how it works.

3. a) The mechanism shown in diagram A is found on bicycles. What is it called?

b) If the large wheel turns through 18 revolutions, how many revolutions will the small wheel turn?

Diagram A

35 teeth   18 teeth

4. a) Name the mechanism shown in diagram B and explain how it works.

Diagram B

b) In what way is the movement of the wheels of the mechanism shown in diagram C different to those in diagram B.

Diagram C

c) What weakness is there with these mechanisms which is not found in the one shown in diagram A?

1. Commercial manufacturing consists of a system or group of sub-systems. Name SIX.

i) ....

ii) ....

iii) ....

iv) ....

v) ....

vi) ....

2. a) Explain what you understand by the term 'Division of Labour.'

....

b) Explain what you understand by the term 'Right first time, every time.'

....

....

3. a) What is Quality Assurance?

....

....

....

....

b) The British Standards Institute (BSI) devise tests with which to check products and components.

   i) What does the symbol shown mean?

....

   ii) If a company displayed 'BS EN ISO 9000 2000' what would it mean?

....

c) Suggest FOUR Quality Control tests which could be carried out on a product as it is made.

i) ....   ii) ....

iii) ....   iv) ....

4. Explain the term 'Working To Tolerance.'

....

....

....

1. Suggest THREE Health and Safety checks you would make before using a drilling machine?

i) ....

ii) ....

iii) ....

2. Suggest THREE ways in which you can help to protect your classmates from Health and Safety risks.

i) ....

ii) ....

iii) ....

3. What would you do if you slipped when using a craft knife and cut your finger deeply?

....

....

....

....

4. A small fire in the school workshop appears to have started from a faulty strip heater.

a) Which of the two extinguishers shown would you expect your teacher to use?

....

b) Why would your teacher use this one?

....

....

....

Black

Red

c) What should you do?

....

....

5. Dust can be a major hazard. Suggest TWO ways in which you can reduce the health risk to ...

a) ... yourself: ....

b) ... others in the room: ....